I0413154

CONTENTS

CORE EXPECTATIONS FOR PEACE CORPS VOLUNTEERS

In working toward fulfilling the Peace Corps mission of promoting world peace and friendship, as a trainee and Volunteer, you are expected to do the following:

1. Prepare your personal and professional life to make a commitment to serve abroad for a full term of 27 months

2. Commit to improving the quality of life of the people with whom you live and work and, in doing so, share your skills, adapt them, and learn new skills as needed

3. Serve where the Peace Corps asks you to go, under conditions of hardship if necessary, and with the flexibility needed for effective service

4. Recognize that your successful and sustainable development work is based on the local trust and confidence you build by living in, and respectfully integrating yourself into, your host community and culture

5. Recognize that you are responsible 24 hours a day, 7 days a week for your personal conduct and professional performance

6. Engage with host country partners in a spirit of cooperation, mutual learning, and respect

7. Work within the rules and regulations of the Peace Corps and the local and national laws of the country where you serve

8. Exercise judgment and personal responsibility to protect your health, safety, and well-being and that of others

9. Recognize that you will be perceived, in your host country and community, as a representative of the people, cultures, values, and traditions of the United States of America

10. Represent responsively the people, cultures, values, and traditions of your host country and community to people in the United States both during and following your service

PEACE CORPS/COSTA RICA HISTORY AND PROGRAMS

History of the Peace Corps in Costa Rica

Since 1963, more than 3,000 Peace Corps Volunteers (PCVs) have served in Costa Rica in a variety of projects in the areas of health, education, the environment, community development, agriculture, small business development, and youth development. Throughout the program's existence, Volunteers have been consistently well received by the Costa Rican people and local partner agencies.

The children, youth, and families (CYF) project was the primary sector of the Peace Corps/Costa Rica program from 1998–2002. In 2003, a second project in rural community development (RCD) began, which focuses on the poorest rural communities in the country. In 2005, a third project in Community Economic Development (CED) began. In 2010, a fourth project began in teaching English as a foreign language (TEFL).

History and Future of Peace Corps Programming in Costa Rica

Peace Corps/Costa Rica (PCCR) celebrates Peace Corps 50th anniversary in Costa Rica in 2013. PCCR has been operating continuously since January 23, 1963, with the arrival of the first group of 26 PCVs who were assigned as English and science teachers to public schools.

- During the Peace Corps' history in Costa Rica, its programs have changed to respond and adapt to the needs and challenges of Costa Rica and its people. Early programs responded to needs in the health and agriculture sectors.
- In the 1970s and '80s, the education sector became a country priority, culminating in the development of a national curriculum on environmental education which the Peace Corps helped pioneer. By the mid 1980s, the Peace Corps started small business and housing projects to assist Costa Rica in the creation of employment opportunities and the construction of new housing units.
- In the 1990s and 2000s, Peace Corps programming changed to more directly support economic development, community education, environmental management, youth development, and, more recently, teaching English as a foreign language (TEFL).

Peace Corps Costa Rica (PCCR) currently has approximately 100 PCVs in-country, and 20 Peace Corps trainees (PCTs). PCVs are assigned to work in communities throughout the country in collaboration with local partners.

Teaching English as a Foreign Language

The TEFL project collaborates closely with Costa Rica Multilingüe (now an independent foundation) and the Ministry of Public Education (MEP) to provide Costa Rican students and teachers personal, professional, and academic opportunities through English. PCV site assignments are made in close consultation with MEP to ensure support is provided where it is most needed and can be most effectively leveraged. PCVs serve primarily as co-planners/co-teachers with MEP English teachers (at both the primary and secondary level) to improve the teaching and learning of English. PCVs also work directly with students to improve their English language proficiency, raise academic success, and develop leadership skills. The TEFL project also brought on two Peace Corps Response Volunteers in 2012 to explore new partnerships, and five in 2013 to strengthen the capacity of National Training Institute (INA) English teachers supporting this vital sector.

Community Economic Development

The Community Economic Development (CED) project works together with national and local public and private sector partners (Ministry of Agriculture and Livestock, Ministry of Science and Technology, Fundación Omar Dengo, FINCA, Intel, etc.) to expand markets, sustain economic growth, and improve the standard of living for families and communities. PCVs are located in rural and semi-rural areas (usually with populations of more than 500) working in the agro-industrial and community based eco-tourism sectors. The project focuses on two goals: improving youth workforce development through training in financial literacy, employability, and vocational skills such as English and information technology; and strengthening economic opportunities through training in entrepreneurship and business management practices and access to business finance.

Youth in Development

The Youth in Development Project (YD) project works together with national public and private sector partners (Costa Rican Child Protection Agency, the MEP's student life sector, Youth Action Foundation, the Costa Rican Demographic Association and the Institute on Alcoholism and Drug Dependency) to empower youth to make informed decisions about their education, health, and lifestyles to assume positive roles in their own development with the support of involved partners and service providers. At the local level, PCVs work with elementary and secondary schools, community development organizations, youth groups and committees, Girl and Boy Scouts, health facilities, and any other organizations that serve youth locally. PCVs are assigned to live in marginal urban and semi-urban areas outside of the central valley that have been recognized as national priorities based on a developmental index measuring the prevalence of poverty, unemployment, and various social problems such as delinquency, drug consumption, school drop-out, and teenage pregnancy. The target populations for this project are children and youth under age 18, given their vulnerability as a demographic group, as well as parents and service providers working with youth. Volunteers support youth and youth service providers through educational and recreational programs that contribute to school retention and mitigate teen pregnancy and drug and alcohol consumption.

Rural Community Development

The Rural Community Development (RCD) project, which began in 2003, closed in May 2013, leaving a 10-year legacy in rural Costa Rican communities. The Peace Corps Volunteers in the RCD project worked closely with national community development agency DINADECO regional representatives to provide technical assistance to strengthen the organizational capacity of community-based organizations (Asociaciones de Desarrollo Integral) committed to local development. RCD Volunteers were placed in sites identified as high priority by DINADECO in the following regions: the Chorotega, Pacífico Central, Brunca, Huetar Norte, and Huetar Atlántica.

COUNTRY OVERVIEW: COSTA RICA AT A GLANCE

History

While there is debate about the number of indigenous people in Costa Rica prior to the arrival of Christopher Columbus in 1502, few survived contact with Europeans. Today, the country's indigenous population makes up less than 2 percent of the total population.

For nearly three centuries, Spain administered what is now Costa Rica as part of the Captaincy General of Guatemala, under a military government. The Spanish optimistically called the country "Rich Coast." Finding little gold or other valuable minerals in Costa Rica, however, the Spanish turned to agriculture. The small landowners' relative poverty, the lack of a large indigenous labor force, the population's ethnic and linguistic homogeneity, and Costa Rica's isolation from the Spanish colonial centers in Mexico and the Andes contributed to the development of a relatively autonomous, individualistic, and egalitarian agrarian society. This tradition survived the widened class distinctions brought on by the introduction of banana and coffee cultivation in the 19th century and the subsequent accumulation of local wealth.

Costa Rica joined other Central American provinces in 1821 in a joint declaration of independence from Spain. In 1838, long after the Central American Federation ceased to function in practice, Costa Rica formally withdrew and proclaimed itself a sovereign nation. An era of peaceful democracy in Costa Rica began in 1899, and has continued through today with only two lapses: 1917–19, when Federico Tinoco ruled as a dictator, and

1948, when Jose Figueres led an armed uprising in the wake of a disputed presidential election. The victorious junta from this 44-day civil war drafted a constitution guaranteeing free elections with universal suffrage and the abolition of the military. Figueres became a national hero, winning the first election under the new constitution in 1953. The lack of a military continues to be a source of great national pride, and Costa Rica is presently conducting an international public relations campaign to encourage other nations to follow suit for the purpose of global peace.

The Costa Rican government has been very involved in managing the economy since the 1948 revolution. The government operates many state monopolies, including banking, insurance, and telecommunications (recently deregulated and now open to competition); controls the prices of a number of goods and services; and maintains protectionist trade laws. Government policy in the 1960s and '70s focused on making Costa Rica more self-sufficient, and the nation has enjoyed a gradual upward economic trend. However, with the increase in oil prices in the 1970s and sharp decreases in international coffee, banana, and sugar prices, Costa Rica's economy collapsed in 1980. Warfare in neighboring countries in the 1980s also affected the Costa Rican economy and society, shattering regional trade and bringing a large number of refugees and illegal aliens, particularly from Nicaragua, to the country. To quell the regional violence, President Oscar Arias Sánchez (1986–90) promoted a successful regional peace plan that resulted in his receipt of the Nobel Peace Prize in 1987. Since 1948, Costa Rica has held 12 successive democratic presidential elections, more than any other Latin American country.

Government

Costa Rica is a democratic republic with strong constitutional checks and balances. Executive responsibilities are vested in a president, who is the country's center of power. There also are two vice presidents and a 15-member cabinet, which includes one of the vice presidents. The president and the 57 Legislative Assembly senators (*diputados*) are elected for four-year terms. Presidents serve four-year terms, but cannot serve them consecutively. An independent Supreme Electoral Tribunal supervises the electoral process. The Supreme Court of Justice exercises judicial power and a chamber of the Supreme Court reviews the constitutionality of legislation, executive decrees, and all habeas corpus warrants.

The offices of the Comptroller General of the Republic (inspector general), Procurator General of the Pubic (attorney general), and Ombudsman exercise autonomous oversight of the government. State agencies enjoy considerable operational independence; they include the telecommunications and electrical power monopoly (Instituto Costarricense de Electricidad), the nationalized commercial banks (Banco Nacional de Costa Rica), the state insurance monopoly (Instituto Nacional de Seguros), and the social security health care agency (Caja Costarricense de Seguro Social). Costa Rica has no military; it maintains police and security forces only for internal security.

The government of Costa Rica has emphasized the development of democracy and respect for human rights throughout its history. Until recently, the country's political system contrasted sharply with those of many of its Central American and Caribbean neighbors. Costa Rica experienced several unusual days of low-level civil disturbance in early 2000 over legislation that would have permitted private-sector participation in the state-owned telecommunications and electrical power sectors.

The elections of February 5, 2006, were historic for several reasons. First, the enduring bipartisanship of the last 50 years between the National Liberation Party (PLN) and Social Christian Unity Party (PUSC) ended as 15 presidential candidates entered the primaries, all of them from different political parties. Second, a 36-year-old law stating a president could not re-run for office was overruled and former president and 1987 Nobel Peace Prize winner Oscar Arias entered the race. Third, the election results were unusually close, with an extremely low voter turnout (an estimated 40 percent of the voting population did not vote due to a lack of trust for the candidates).

Arias was re-elected president with 41.1 percent of the popular vote; Oton Solis of Civil Action Party (PAC) had 40 percent of the vote. (In Costa Rica, a candidate must receive at least 40 percent of the vote to win the election. If none of them had reached 40 percent of the votes, a second round would have been necessary.) During the campaign, Solis was a firm opponent to the Central American Free Trade Agreement (CAFTA), while Arias defended its approval and stated it was a priority for his administration.

The 2006 legislative elections saw significant gains in seats by diverse political parties. This phenomenon has continued in subsequent elections, making it imperative for the majority party, PLN, to form legislative coalitions in order to advance its political agenda. This distribution forced PLN to negotiate with the minority representatives to pass CAFTA. Costa Rica was the last signatory of all Central American nations for the CAFTA agreement. Although a popular vote (the first national referendum) was carried out on October 5, 2007, and the people of Costa Rica voted to implement CAFTA in their country by a slim majority of 51.62 percent in favor and 48.38 percent against, government officials continue to struggle with the implementation of the agreement. The division of political parties continues to reflect greatly in the negotiations of CAFTA at the government level. Although CAFTA was voted in by the people, the constitution needs to be changed in order for CAFTA to be fully implemented. This process is still ongoing.

In Febraury 2010, after a hard-fought campaign, Costa Rica elected its first female president, Laura Chinchilla, the candidate of the PLN Party. She took office in a momentous inauguration ceremony in La Sabana Park in San José on May 8, 2010. President Chinchilla was a vice president under President Arias in his second term, and a former minister of security. She ran on a platform focused on safeguarding citizen security, promoting transparency in government, and bringing equitable development to underserved areas of the country. The legislature remains divided between several political parties, requiring political alliances to advance executive and legislative agendas.

The next presidential election will be held in February 2014. Candidates from various parties are already campaigning. The PLN candidate (the same party as Arias and Chinchilla) is Johnny Araya, the mayor of San Jose. Given the current, fractious political environment, it will be a very contentious campaign season and a highly competitive presidential election.

Economy

After a very difficult economic crisis during 2007–09, when annual inflation rates were near 14 percent, the highest in the last 15 years, Costa Rica's economy has begun to stabilize. The 2012 inflation rate ended at 4.55 percent. A similar inflation rate is expected for 2013. Real growth rate for 2012 was at 5 percent and unemployment was close to 10 percent. As of May 2013, the exchange rate hovered near 500 colóns to the dollar.

Costa Rica's major economic resources are its fertile land and frequent rainfall, well-educated population, and attractive ecological diversity. Its location in the Central American isthmus provides easy access to North and South American markets and direct ocean access to Europe and Asia. The economy of Costa Rica has been dependent on the production and export of bananas and coffee. While these products, along with sugar cane and beef, are still important, tourism, manufacturing, and services have surpassed agriculture's contribution to gross domestic product and diversified the economy. Costa Rica has also successfully attracted important foreign investments in free-trade zones by large international companies. Tourism is booming and now earns more foreign exchange than bananas and coffee combined. The government still holds controlling interests in many sectors of the economy, particularly in telecommunications, electricity, water supply, and banking. Costa Rica continues to strive to widen economic and trade ties both within and outside the region.

Nearly one-quarter of Costa Ricans live below the poverty line and the gap between the rich and poor continues to widen. Therefore, while you will see visible affluence, including modern shopping malls, newly released American movies, well-developed tourist resorts, and the latest-model cars on the streets of San Jose, you will live and work with people who do not have access to such privileges.

People and Culture

Costa Ricans, commonly known as *ticos*, are predominantly of Spanish descent. There are smaller groups of people of Afro-Caribbean (3 percent), indigenous AmerIndian (1.7 percent), and Asian heritage (1 percent). Costa Rica also hosts many refugees, mainly from Colombia and Nicaragua. Migrants from Nicaragua make up nearly 10 percent of the population. Spanish is the national language, although many people on the Caribbean coast speak English and Patois (a form of Creole English). The population of Costa Rica is approximately 4.2 million; 59 percent are urban and 41 percent are rural, with more and more people moving to urban areas. Most people belong to the Roman Catholic Church (70 percent), which is the constitutionally declared national religion, although congregations of Evangelical churches are growing (14 percent). The last official census took place in 2011.

Costa Rica boasts a relatively high literacy rate (by some counts, as high as 96 percent). According to UNICEF, attendance at elementary schools (up to sixth grade) is approximately 80 percent. However, attendance drops significantly (to 65 percent) at the secondary-school level, and only 35 percent of those who begin high school actually graduate. Infant mortality in Costa Rica is low (9.9 percent) relative to that of its neighbors, and its life expectancy is comparable to that in the United States. Teenage mothers account for 20 percent of all births.

Environment

The Republic of Costa Rica is located in Central America, with Panama to the south, Nicaragua to the north, the Caribbean Sea to the east, and the Pacific Ocean to the west. It covers a land area of 19,652 square miles—about the size of West Virginia. A chain of volcanic mountains runs through the center of the country into Nicaragua, splitting Costa Rica in two. In the center of the mountain ranges is a high-altitude plain, with coastal lowlands on either side. Much of the country was once covered with dense forests and jungles, most of which have been cut down to provide farmland. There has been a concerted effort to preserve what is left by the creation of a national park system, which covers almost 12 percent of the country, and forest reserves and indigenous reservations boost the protected land area to 27 percent. Costa Rica is famous for its great diversity of tropical flora and fauna.

While strong legislation exists for these protected areas, enforcement has been a problem and illegal poaching and logging occur. Outside the protected areas, Costa Rica faces a wide range of environmental challenges, including poor solid waste management, lack of water treatment facilities, deforestation, air pollution from vehicles and industry, noise pollution, coastal degradation, and the ever-increasing development of tourist areas.

RESOURCES FOR FURTHER INFORMATION

Following is a list of websites for additional information about the Peace Corps and Costa Rica and to connect you to returned Volunteers and other invitees. Please keep in mind that the Peace Corps cannot guarantee that the these links are active and current. If you do not have access to the Internet, visit your local library. Libraries offer free Internet usage and often let you print information to take home.

A note of caution: As you surf the Internet, be aware that you may find bulletin boards and chat rooms in which people are free to express opinions about the Peace Corps based on their own experience, including comments by those who were unhappy with their choice to serve in the Peace Corps. These opinions are not those of the Peace Corps or the U.S. government, and please keep in mind that no two people experience their service in the same way.

General Information About Costa Rica

www.lonelyplanet.com/destinations
Visit this site for general travel advice about almost any country in the world.

www.state.gov
The Department of State's website issues background notes periodically about countries around the world. Find Costa Rica and learn more about its social and political history. You can also go to the site's international travel section to check on conditions that may affect your safety.

www.geography.about.com/library/maps/blindex.htm
This online world atlas includes maps and geographical information, and each country page contains links to other sites, such as the Library of Congress, that contain comprehensive historical, social, and political background.

www.cyberschoolbus.un.org/infonation/info.asp
This United Nations site allows you to search for statistical information for member states of the U.N.

Connect With Returned Volunteers and Other Invitees

www.rpcv.org
This is the site of the National Peace Corps Association, made up of returned Volunteers. On this site you can find links to all the Web pages of the "Friends of" groups for most countries of service, comprised of former Volunteers who served in those countries. There are also regional groups that frequently get together for social events and local volunteer activities.

www.PeaceCorpsWorldwide.org
This site is hosted by a group of returned Volunteer writers. It is a monthly online publication of essays and Volunteer accounts of their Peace Corps service.

Online Articles/Current News Sites About Costa Rica

www.ticotimes.net
Tico Times, an English-language weekly

www.nacion.com
La Nación, a daily newspaper in Spanish

http://www.larepublica.net
La República, a daily newspaper in Spanish

www.amcostarica.com
A.M. Costa Rica, a daily English-language summary of Costa Rican news

www.semanario.ucr.ac.cr
El Seminario, a weekly (in Spanish) published by the University of Costa Rica

www.estadonacion.or.cr
An annual analysis (in Spanish) of Costa Rica's most recent socioeconomic and environmental indicators

www.flacso.org
The site of Facultad Latinoamericana de Ciencias Sociales, a social science research organization (in Spanish)

International Development Sites About Costa Rica

www.nu.or.cr
United Nations programs, including UNDP, UNICEF, UNFPA, and UNESCO, in Costa Rica

http://www.oas.org/
Organization of American States

www.iadb.org
Inter-American Development Bank

http://www.paho.org/English/DD/AIS/cp_188.htm
Pan American Health Organization in Costa Rica

Recommended Books

1. Booth, John. "Costa Rica: Quest for Democracy." Boulder, CO: Westview Press, 1998.

2. Brendtro, Brokenleg, Van Bockern. "Reclaiming Youth At Risk: Our Hope for the Future," Bloomington, IN: National Educational Service, 1990.

2. Daling, Tjabel. "Costa Rica in Focus: A Guide to the People, Politics, and Culture." London: Latin America Bureau, 1998.

3. Edelman, Marc, and Joanne Kenen (eds.). "The Costa Rican Reader." New York: Grove Press, 1989.

4. Lara, Silvia, et al. "Inside Costa Rica: The Essential Guide to Its Politics, Economy, Society, and Environment." Silver City, NM: Interhemispheric Resource Center, 1995.

5. Mavis, Hiltunen Biesanz, et al. "The Ticos: Culture and Social Change in Costa Rica." Boulder, CO: Lynne Rienner Publishers, 1998.

6. Molina, Iván, and Steven Palmer. "The History of Costa Rica." San José, Costa Rica: Editorial de la Universidad de Costa Rica, 1998.

7. Ras, Barbara, and Oscar Arias (eds.). "Costa Rica: A Traveler's Literary Companion." St. Paul: Consortium Book Sales, 1994. Translations of 26 short stories by 20 of Costa Rica's best authors.

8. Van Rheenen, Erin. "Living Abroad in Costa Rica." Emerville, CA: Avalon Publishing Group, Inc. 2004.

Books About the History of the Peace Corps

1. Hoffman, Elizabeth Cobbs. "All You Need is Love: The Peace Corps and the Spirit of the 1960s." Cambridge, MA: Harvard University Press, 2000.

2. Rice, Gerald T. "The Bold Experiment: JFK's Peace Corps." Notre Dame, IN: University of Notre Dame Press, 1985.

3. Stossel, Scott. "Sarge: The Life and Times of Sargent Shriver." Washington, DC: Smithsonian Institution Press, 2004.

4. Meisler, Stanley. "When the World Calls: The Inside Story of the Peace Corps and its First 50 Years." Boston: Beacon Press, 2011.

Books on the Volunteer Experience

1. Dirlam, Sharon. "Beyond Siberia: Two Years in a Forgotten Place." Santa Barbara, CA: McSeas Books, 2004.

2. Casebolt, Marjorie DeMoss. "Margarita: A Guatemalan Peace Corps Experience." Gig Harbor, WA: Red Apple Publishing, 2000.

3. Erdman, Sarah. "Nine Hills to Nambonkaha: Two Years in the Heart of an African Village." New York City: Picador, 2003.

4. Hessler, Peter. "River Town: Two Years on the Yangtze." New York City: Perennial, 2001.

5. Kennedy, Geraldine ed. "From the Center of the Earth: Stories out of the Peace Corps." Santa Monica, CA: Clover Park Press, 1991.

6. Thompsen, Moritz. "Living Poor: A Peace Corps Chronicle." Seattle: University of Washington Press, 1997 (reprint).

LIVING CONDITIONS AND VOLUNTEER LIFESTYLE

Communications

Mail

Airmail to and from Costa Rica takes one to two weeks. Volunteers in more remote areas of the country will likely have additional delays. You can receive mail at the Peace Corps office during training and as a Volunteer.

The mailing address of the Peace Corps office is as follows:
"Your Name," PCT
Cuerpo de Paz
Apartado Postal 1266-1000
San Jose, Costa Rica

Once you have completed training, you will be responsible for sending the address of your new site to friends and family members. Most sites are near post offices, and a Volunteer can rent a post office box or have mail delivered directly to his or her home. You may also choose to maintain the Peace Corps office as your mailing address. You will decide that once you are assigned to your new site.

Do not have people send you money, airline tickets, or other valuable items through the mail. Items mailed in padded manila envelopes have a better chance of arriving at your site without being delayed by customs. Larger packages have to go through customs and sometimes disappear in transit. Retrieving packages from customs is time-consuming and most often requires payment of duty fees and storage charges that are sometimes more than the value of what is in your package.

DHL, FedEx, and other couriers have offices in Costa Rica. If your friends or relatives want to send you something by courier, they should send it to the Peace Corps office, for which a phone number and directions to a street address are usually required. Please be aware that if you are sent something by such couriers there is often a charge in which you, the trainee/Volunteer, are responsible for paying in order to receive the package. The Peace Corps/Costa Rica office phone number is 011.506.2231.4122; the fax number is 011.506.2231.4122 ext. 132. The Peace Corps/Costa Rica office address follows:

"Your Name," PCT
Boulevard Rohrmoser
300 m. Oeste de la Farmacia Fischel
El Triangula Costado Oeste del Parque La Loma
La Favorita, Pavas
San Jose, Costa Rica

Telephones

International phone service to and from Costa Rica is good. Direct calls to the United States can be made at Internet cafes for a small fee and most public phones will allow you to make international calls using a calling card (e.g., AT&T, Sprint, or the Costa Rican telephone company) or by calling collect. Many houses have landlines through which Volunteers can receive calls from the States. Many international calling cards purchased in the United States do not work in Costa Rica. It is recommended that you purchase phone cards in Costa Rica to ensure they are compatible with local phone services. Many Volunteers use the Internet phone services from personal computers or Internet cafes as a means of making inexpensive international phone calls to family and friends.

During training, most of the Volunteers' host families have telephones; if they do not, there is likely to be a neighbor with a phone or a public phone nearby. Telephone service is more limited at a few rural sites. Many Volunteers choose to purchase their own cellphones or activate cellphones that they bring with them from the States; Peace Corps/Costa Rica does not provide Volunteers with cellphones. You do not need a cellular phone to carry out your work in Costa Rica but it is recommended you have one for your security. Most U.S. cellphones are not compatible with the cellular technology in Costa Rica; in order for a cellphone purchased in the States to work in Costa Rica it must be unblocked. The telephone service used to be a monopoly governed by the state. As a result of CAFTA, the service was recently privatized and is now open to competition. Though the market is constantly evolving, there are now more options for trainees and Volunteers to purchase cellphones and secure lines in Costa Rica.

Fax service is also available in most cities, usually at the local post office. The post office charges a fee for both sending and receiving faxes. Once you are at your assigned site, you can send a fax number to your friends and relatives for easier communication.

To reach you in an emergency, your family can call the Office of Counseling and Outreach (COU) at Peace Corps/headquarters in Washington, D.C., at 855.855.1961 ext. 1470. The COU will contact Peace Corps/Costa Rica as soon as possible to relay the information.

Computer, Internet, and Email Access

You will have access to computers and the Internet at the Volunteer resource center at the Peace Corps office in San José once you are sworn in a Peace Corps Volunteer. You will not have access to the resource center computers as a trainee. The majority of Volunteers have weekly, if not daily, access to Internet in their sites. However, Volunteers placed in rural sites generally have more limited communication options and access in their sites. Bringing a personal computer to Costa Rica may increase your risk of being a victim of theft. Nevertheless, the overwhelming majority of Volunteers bring laptop computers and find them useful for work, entertainment, and communication purposes. If you choose to bring a laptop computer, it is strongly recommended that you purchase personal articles insurance to protect yourself from theft. Wi-Fi access is available in some Volunteer sites through a portable device that can be purchased and requires a monthly fee or is available free of charge with personal computers in the Peace Corps office.

Housing and Site Location

Currently, there are Volunteers in all parts of the country: the Central Valley, Limón on the Caribbean Coast, Puntarenas on the Pacific Coast, as far north as Los Chiles near the Nicaraguan border, and as far south as Paso Canoas on the Panamá border. While sites vary in size, climate, and distance to downtown San José (from two hours to 10 hours by bus), each has been preselected by the Peace Corps in consultation with relevant host country agencies for their potential to offer a Volunteer meaningful work opportunities consistent with the project and community support.

The profile of the living conditions for Volunteers varies greatly in the different projects. Volunteers in the YD project live in urban, semi-urban, and occasionally rural communities. Some YD sites are converted squatter settlements composed of a combination of tin and wooden shacks, but most sites have recently built two- or three-room cement block buildings with corrugated steel roofs. Volunteers in semi-urban sites have access, via a short bus ride, to services such as banking, postal, and hospital care.

Community profiles for the CED and TEFL projects are more likely to be semi-urban to semi-rural (more than 500 inhabitants) towns. Again, Volunteers in these sites have access, via a short bus ride, to services such as banking, postal, and hospital care.

All Volunteer houses have cold running water and electricity, and most have phones. In all communities, you will find a church, a school, and general stores (*pulperías*) that sell staples such as rice, black beans, tuna, soap, soft drinks, and snack food.

During training, you will live with a family selected by the training staff in one of several training communities. Your living conditions in training will likely be of a higher standard than that of your house in your site.

During your first six months of service, you are also **required** to live with a family in your assigned community. This promotes your integration into the community, allows you to live as the majority of Costa Ricans do, increases your language skills, and helps ensure your safety and security. The families to which you are assigned are recommended by community leaders or by your partner agency. These families are provided an orientation by your program manager and, sometimes, a currently serving Volunteer. Requests to live independently after the first six months at site are approved on a case-by-case basis, depending on available, affordable housing that meets PC/Costa Rica's safety and security requirements and based upon the level of integration and Spanish communication skills that a Volunteer has achieved.

The family with whom you stay is likely to have children, and their home will be modest in size and comfort. While the Peace Corps requests that Volunteers be given their own room, you may find that its walls do not reach the ceiling or are very thin. The concept of individual space in Costa Rica is different from that in the United States. While some Volunteers find living with a family frustrating at times, they also concede that it is an enriching way to experience a new culture and develop an awareness of its values.

While you will find most Costa Rican people to be kind and good, some community members may struggle with a variety of problems, including substance abuse and alcoholism, low income, single parenthood, child abuse, high unemployment, delinquency, lack of organization, etc. Therefore, your safety is a major concern, and you will have to adjust and conform to different norms of behavior and take continual precautions to maximize your safety. The Health Care and Safety section provides more information on this important issue.

Living Allowance and Money Management

During pre-service training, the Peace Corps will open an electronic debit account (in colóns) for you at Banco Nacional, to which you can gain access from any of the bank's automated teller machines throughout the country (most ATM cards from U.S. banks can also be used at local banks, with a service fee), as well as online at www.bncr.fi.cr. The debit card can also be used at most larger businesses. The Peace Corps pays host families a set amount to cover your food, lodging, and laundry during training and deposits a small walk-around allowance in your account for incidental expenses.

When you become a Volunteer, the Peace Corps will begin depositing a living allowance in your account each month, along with a one-time settling-in allowance to purchase items to set up your home. The amount of the living allowance is based on an annual cost-of-living survey of current Volunteers and is intended to cover all of your essential expenses, including rent, local travel, food, and entertainment. You will negotiate the rent you pay your host family using guidelines provided by the Peace Corps.

It is important to maintain a lifestyle similar to that of the people with whom you live and work, so you do not need to bring additional money. Nevertheless, many Volunteers bring at least one major credit card in case they need to make a major personal purchase or for out-of-country travel. If you choose to bring extra money, bringing traveler's checks or opening a local bank account in dollars will minimize the risk of loss or theft. You will also accrue $24 per month of Volunteer service for a vacation allowance, deposited monthly in your account in local currency.

Food and Diet

During training, you will typically eat three meals a day, prepared by, and shared with, your host family. You are treated as a member of the family, not as a guest. As such, families are not expected to prepare special meals for you. Once you are a Volunteer, you can arrange to have all or some of your meals with your host family or buy and prepare your own food.

The availability of fresh fruits and vegetables depends on the season and the region in which you will reside. Costa Ricans tend to eat few green vegetables, favoring root vegetables (potatoes, sweet potatoes, cassavas, etc.). Volunteers sometimes comment on the lack of diversity in the local diet, which relies heavily on rice and beans and starchy foods fried in oil or lard. The training team meets with each family and provides a brief orientation. During this orientation, the Peace Corps staff emphasizes to families the concern of cooking with too much oil or lard. In most cases this advice is followed, but Peace Corps cannot mandate how a family should cook. Remember, this is why you joined the Peace Corps: to integrate into a family and community, living as they do. Many families do not eat a lot of meat because of its high cost. Although nearly any specialty food can be purchased at supermarkets in San José, these imported products are not part of the local diet and are well beyond the economic means of most host families.

It is relatively easy for vegetarians to maintain their diet in Costa Rica, since rice and beans are the staple foods. However, Costa Ricans often prepare their vegetables with meat or in meat broth, so you will have to make special arrangements to maintain a strictly vegetarian diet. In addition, Volunteers should not expect families to purchase additional foods outside of their normal purchases to compensate for your eating requirements.

Transportation

Costa Rica has an extensive road system of more than 18,600 miles (30,000 km). Although much of it is in disrepair, there is access to almost any spot in Costa Rica by means of a vehicle. The main cities in the Central Valley are connected by paved, all-weather roads to the Caribbean and Pacific coasts and to the Pan American Highway, which goes to Nicaragua and Panama, Costa Rica's neighbors to the north and south. Unfortunately, the rate of traffic-related fatalities is one of the highest per capita in the world.

Volunteers travel mainly by public bus. Costa Rica has an extensive, dependable bus system that operates in most of the country. The service is inexpensive and usually runs on a set schedule several times a day. In the San José metropolitan area, however, traffic jams often extend travel times.

The Peace Corps requires PCVs to travel in "official" taxis; the red cars with yellow triangles on the front doors are easily identifiable. Most fares within the San José area are determined by using the meter (called the maría), but longer distances are usually set at a fixed rate.

Volunteers are not allowed to drive motorized vehicles except during an official vacation and with a valid Costa Rican or international driver's license. Some Volunteers request permission to purchase a bicycle to facilitate travel around their sites. You must wear a bicycle helmet provided by the Peace Corps whenever you ride. Volunteers are not allowed to drive or ride on motorcycles.

Geography and Climate

There are two distinct seasons in Costa Rica: rainy and dry. In much of the country, the rainy season lasts from May to November, but parts of the Caribbean Coast receive rain year-round. And when it rains, heavy afternoon downpours are common, resulting in flooded or muddy streets. The driest months in San José are December through April. The southwestern plains and mountain slopes receive more rain, averaging only three dry months a year. Temperatures vary little between seasons and the main influence on temperature is altitude.

San José, at almost 3,800 feet (1,150 meters) above sea level, has temperatures between 60–80 degrees Fahrenheit. The coasts and lowlands are much hotter, averaging 72 F at night and 86 F during the day. Although this is a general description of weather patterns, ever-changing climate changes continue to affect Costa Rica's "normal" seasons.

Training takes place in several communities in the Central Valley, so be prepared for warm days and cool nights. You will need a warm jacket or heavy sweater during training, especially during the rainy season, when the dampness and wind make it quite chilly. During training, host families will provide bedding appropriate to the climate. A blanket (easily purchased in Costa Rica) is necessary for sleeping, even at lower altitudes.

The climate at your future worksite will depend on where you are located. You should be prepared for a location that is very hot, somewhat cooler, or anything in between.

Social Activities

Since your assignment will entail working with people, much of your "work" time will be spent socializing and getting to know community members by drinking a *cafecito* (coffee) with them. This time with community members is important to build the trust necessary to work effectively with them. The Peace Corps expects Volunteers to spend most evenings and weekends working or socializing in their community, except when they work in another community on integrated programming efforts.

Most Volunteers celebrate birthdays, weddings, and holidays with their host families. Other activities depend on the size of the community. Smaller sites have activities at the community center, local school, soccer field, and churches. Larger communities may also have restaurants, a movie theater, a dance hall or disco, and special cultural activities. When you are in San José, you will find a variety of movie theaters, music and theater performances, art galleries, museums, and sports events. In addition, you are likely to discover places of incredible natural beauty close to your site and throughout the country.

Professionalism, Dress, and Behavior

As a novelty in your community, you will be noticed, and your dress and behavior will be commented upon. Therefore, to minimize any unnecessary obstacles in your work and personal relations, you must respect local cultural norms. To help ensure that you serve as a positive role model by working in a professional and ethical manner, you will be asked to sign a copy of the Code of Behavior that governs the Peace Corps program in Costa Rica.

Personal appearance delivers a message, whether intended or unintended. As in the United States, dressing appropriately and professionally in Costa Rica can enhance your credibility, since it reflects your respect for the customs and expectations of the people with whom you live and work. Inappropriate dress, like inappropriate behavior, is something that can set you unnecessarily apart from your community. Until you become well-known by Costa Ricans, your dress will be an important indicator to them. From the biggest city to the most remote village, you will be judged, especially initially, on your appearance.

Costa Ricans dress very neatly and take great pride in looking good in public (e.g., clean and ironed clothes, polished shoes, and groomed hair), even on informal occasions. "Dressing down" is not a common phenomenon, since status is measured in part by appearance. For example, it may be confusing and offensive for them to see a "rich" North American wear dirty gym shoes or informal flip-flops when dressier shoes are appropriate. Volunteers will gain greater acceptance of their ideas by wearing the right outfit, which generally means dressing in a professional manner (it's suggested you dress how one would in the United States in a similar situation). For example, in schools, Costa Rican women tend to wear skirts, dresses, or pressed pants; men tend to wear collared shirts with pants. A Volunteer should never go into a school or official partner agency office wearing shorts or flip-flops. When visiting with neighbors, however, you can wear casual clothes. You are expected to observe these guidelines for dress during pre-service training as well. You are not coming to Costa Rica on a camping trip; you are moving here for two years to live and work as a development professional. Please bring business-casual clothes for professional settings and comfortable casual clothes for recreational settings.

In most areas of the country, shorts are acceptable for doing household chores, recreational, or sports activities, and spending leisure time in your community. Shorts may not be worn at the Peace Corps office or in other professional settings such as schools, your project partner's office, etc. (long culottes are acceptable for women). In hot areas, women often wear tank tops, sundresses, and dressy sandals for work. Note that sport/outdoor sandals of any brand are not appropriate for work situations in an office or school. Men do not typically wear open-toed sandals of any kind.

Personal Safety

More detailed information about the Peace Corps' approach to safety is contained in the Health Care and Safety section, but it is an important issue and cannot be overemphasized. As stated in the Volunteer Handbook, becoming a Peace Corps Volunteer entails certain safety risks. Living and traveling in an unfamiliar environment (oftentimes alone), having a limited understanding of local language and culture, and being perceived as well-off are some of the factors that can put a Volunteer at risk. Many Volunteers experience varying degrees of unwanted attention and harassment. Petty thefts and burglaries are not uncommon, and incidents of physical and sexual assault do occur, although most Costa Rica Volunteers complete their two years of service without incident. The Peace Corps has established procedures and policies designed to help you reduce your risks and enhance your safety and security. These procedures and policies, in addition to safety training, will be provided once you arrive in Costa Rica. Using these tools, you are expected to take responsibility for your safety and well-being.

Each staff member at the Peace Corps is committed to providing Volunteers with the support they need to successfully meet the challenges they will face to have a safe, healthy, and productive service. Volunteers and families are encouraged to look at the safety and security information on the Peace Corps website at www.peacecorps.gov/safety.

Information on these pages gives messages on Volunteer health and safety. There is a section titled Safety and Security in Depth. Among topics addressed are the risks of serving as a Volunteer, posts' safety support systems, and emergency planning and communications.

Rewards and Frustrations

The Peace Corps is not for everyone. You will have to cope with the frustrations of working in a new culture with different norms and behaviors, and perhaps initially with little Spanish. You may be teased because of your differences from Costa Ricans. You must be willing to live with a family, even though it may make you feel controlled by your host parents. Since a Peace Corps Volunteer's work often extends beyond the hours of a standard workday, and may include weekends, you may feel like you never leave your work. You will work with government employees who are often overworked and underappreciated. The work can be mentally and physically stressful because of Costa Rica's complex social issues. Resources may be limited and facilities inadequate. You will need to have patience and find inner reserves of strength to continue your work with enthusiasm and develop new ideas. In most cases, you will structure your own time. You must possess the self-confidence and vision to continue working toward longterm goals without always seeing immediate results.

You will find that the key to satisfying work as a Peace Corps Volunteer is the ability to establish successful relationships at all levels (with your host family, community members with whom you work, project partner agencies and school officials, and fellow Volunteers). You can expect Costa Ricans to be friendly and, for the most part, interested in having you in their community. You will acquire a sense of accomplishment when small projects are effective due to your efforts. In addition, acceptance into a foreign culture and acquisition of a second (or even a third) language are significant rewards. If you have the personal qualifications needed to meet the challenges of two years of service in Costa Rica, you will have a rewarding, enriching, and lasting experience. You will have the satisfaction of knowing that you have had a positive impact on other people's lives while making much-needed contributions to the goals of Peace Corps/Costa Rica. Judging by the experience of former Volunteers, the rewards are well worth the difficult times, and most Volunteers leave Costa Rica feeling that they gained much more than they sacrificed during their service.

PEACE CORPS TRAINING

Overview of Pre-Service Training

Upon arrival, you will participate in pre-service training (PST), which consists of 12 weeks of intensive in-country preparation in five major areas: Spanish language, technical job orientation, cross-cultural adaptation, health, and safety and security. This integrated program has been designed around the competencies you will need to be successful during your service. To swear in as a Volunteer, you must demonstrate that you have developed the knowledge, skills, and attitudes necessary to meet specific learning objectives. Training is demanding; you will have several assignments, tasks, readings, field visits, and group projects. The Peace Corps evaluates your commitment and performance throughout PST.

Your first PST activity is a four-day orientation retreat immediately upon arrival in-country. During this retreat you will receive detailed information on how PST is carried out (curriculum, methodology, qualification criteria, etc.) and what you can expect for the following 12 weeks (overview and weekly schedules). You will also be required to take the Language Proficiency Interview (LPI), a standardized test to determine your level of proficiency in Spanish.

To most closely assimilate the experience of life and work as a Volunteer, Peace Corps/Costa Rica uses a community-based training (CBT) model. After the retreat, you will be separated into small groups (four or five trainees) according to your language level and assigned to different training communities where you will live with a host family for the following 12 weeks. The experience in the training communities will provide you with an introduction to Costa Rican life and culture and should be seen as a transition to the more challenging sites to which you will be assigned for your service.

CBT allows you to confront and develop strategies to manage work and daily living challenges in a real world context. You will live, train, and integrate into communities, develop relationships, work with community members, and negotiate day-to-day interactions in a new culture and language. The homestay is one of the most valuable aspects of PST. Through this experience you will experience Costa Rican customs, values, routines, diet, and humor firsthand.

During PST, the Peace Corps uses a participatory, experiential approach to learning, known as nonformal education (NFE), which you are expected to use with community members. The NFE methodology helps people build on their own strengths, take charge of their lives, and address their expressed needs. In this way, NFE contributes to achieve Peace Corps' goal of sustainable development.

Training activities will consist of self-directed learning activities, hands-on practice, group sessions, workshops, and field visits. There will be a combination of individual, small group, and large group work. The training curriculum is organized around weekly themes and you can expect to carry out several integrated activities each week. Approximately one day a week, you will meet for technical training in a community facility with the other trainees from your project. For core sessions, all project groups will meet periodically at a larger training hub with easy access from all training communities.

While the majority of PST activities take place in the training communities, there are also three field activities. The first field activity is the **PCV Visit,** during which each trainee is assigned to one Volunteer. You will travel independently for a four-day visit to a current Volunteer site to gather firsthand knowledge of the Volunteer lifestyle. The second field activity is **Tech Week,** during which a small group of trainees travels to one Volunteer's site. You will travel with your project group for a five-day visit to a Volunteer site to practice implementing activities related to your project. The third field activity is the **Site Visit.** This is an independent five-day trip to your future site to meet your project partner and host family, and to get acquainted with the community.

Note to married couples: In order to take full advantage of pre-service training, couples may be separated during specific training events (e.g., Spanish classes, technical activities, visits, etc.). To the degree the couple can be treated as two individuals, by respecting individual learning styles, personalities, interests, strengths, challenges, motivation, and expectations, the Peace Corps is best able to meet the optimal training and service goals for each. If a couple is invited to serve in two different projects, each will live in a different community and will be allowed to spend weekends together at each other's respective host family home. If both are invited to the same project, but with different language levels, you may be able to live together in the same community and one of you will travel daily to another community for the appropriate Spanish class. Also, please note that while couples will be traveling together for PCV and site visits, you may be sent to different locations during Tech Week. Maturity, flexibility, and a true commitment to the training process is critical to a couple's success during this time.

Technical Training

Technical training will prepare you to work in Costa Rica by building on the skills you already have and helping you develop new skills in a manner appropriate to the needs of the country. The Peace Corps staff, Costa Rica experts, and current Volunteers will conduct the training program. Training places great emphasis on learning how to transfer the skills you have to the community in which you will serve as a Volunteer.

Technical training will include sessions on the general economic and political environment in Costa Rica and strategies for working within such a framework. You will review your technical sector's goals and will meet with the Costa Rican agencies and organizations that invited the Peace Corps to assist them. You will be supported and evaluated throughout the training to build the confidence and skills you need to undertake your project activities and be a productive member of your community.

Each project area has a specific technical training curriculum to be followed by all trainees, regardless of your prior professional experience. There are also "core" technical sessions that address cross-sectoral themes and are designed for trainees in all three projects. The goal of the technical training program is not to turn you into an expert in the field, but to assist you in understanding the conditions under which you will work and the resources you will have in Costa Rica. It will provide you with the basic tools to assist you in your first three months of service. You can expect your technical training to be participatory, dynamic, and to require a great deal of self-guided study and hands-on practice.

Language Training

As a Peace Corps Volunteer, you will find that language skills are key to personal and professional satisfaction during your service. These skills are critical to your job performance, they help you integrate into your community, and they can ease your personal adaptation to the new surroundings. Therefore, language training is at the heart of the training program. You must successfully meet minimum language requirements to complete training and become a Volunteer. Costa Rican language instructors teach formal language classes five days a week in small groups of four to five people.

Your language training will incorporate a community-based approach. In addition to classroom time, you will be given assignments to work on outside of the classroom and with your host family. The goal is to get you to a point of basic social communication skills so you can practice and develop language skills further once you are at your site. Prior to being sworn in as a Volunteer, you will work on strategies to continue language studies during your service.

Spanish classes take place in small groups in each training community. Language is not only learned in the classroom, but also by living with a family, integrating into a community, and carrying out assigned tasks. The importance of language ability in your future role as a Volunteer cannot be emphasized enough. Your ability to transfer information, to serve as a community resource and a grassroots development facilitator, as well as your integration into Costa Rican culture, are all directly related to your ability to communicate in the local language. Although language training is provided in-country, you are strongly urged to initiate Spanish language studies before your departure. This will help you meet the criteria to qualify in the language area. Language learning requires dedication and hard work; the vast majority of trainees are able to reach the proficiency level that is required to swear in as a Volunteer.

Cross-Cultural Training

As part of your pre-service training, you will live with a Costa Rican host family. This experience is designed to ease your transition to life at your site. Families go through an orientation conducted by Peace Corps staff to explain the purpose of pre-service training and to assist them in helping you adapt to living in Costa Rica. Many Volunteers form strong and lasting friendships with their host families.

Cross-cultural and community development training will help you improve your communication skills and understand your role as a facilitator of development. You will be exposed to topics such as community mobilization, conflict resolution, gender and development, nonformal and adult education strategies, and political structures.

This component is designed to walk you through the different adaptation challenges that you will most likely face during your first three months in Costa Rica. Being required to live with a host family during pre-service training is the core of your cross-cultural training; it is an authentic way to observe and experience day-to-day living aspects of the Costa Rican culture. During the cross-cultural sessions, you will generate meaningful cross-cultural learning by debriefing your experiences and examining how your own behaviors, beliefs, and values affect how you adapt to Costa Rican culture.

Health Training

During pre-service training, you will be given basic medical training and information. You will be expected to practice preventive health care and to take responsibility for your own health by adhering to all medical policies. Trainees are required to attend all medical sessions. The topics include preventive health measures and minor and major medical issues that you might encounter while in Costa Rica. Nutrition, mental health, setting up a safe living compound, and how to avoid HIV/AIDS and other sexually transmitted infections (STIs) are also covered.

Safety Training

During the safety training sessions, you will learn how to adopt a lifestyle that reduces your risks at home, at work, and during your travels. You will also learn appropriate, effective strategies for coping with unwanted attention and about your individual responsibility for promoting safety throughout your service.

A Volunteer's safety and security is of the utmost concern for the Peace Corps. Safety and security training is designed to raise awareness of the potential risks you might encounter as a trainee/Volunteer and to develop strategies to mitigate them. The Peace Corps has a safety and security coordinator who is responsible for training you on the most common security risks in Costa Rica, strategies to mitigate risk, protocols to follow when your safety or security is compromised, and steps to take in the case of an emergency, etc. Since safety and security is an integral part of everyday life while learning to live in a new country and culture, you will also address safety and security issues with your host family and in your Spanish and cross-cultural sessions. By the end of pre-service training, you are expected to demonstrate that you are prepared and committed to manage your personal safety, as well as to follow all safety and security procedures, as determined by Peace Corps/Costa Rica safety policies and regulations.

Throughout PST, you are encouraged to continue examining your personal motivation for having joined the Peace Corps, as well as your level of dedication and commitment. In this way, when you swear in as a Peace Corps Volunteer, you are making an informed and serious commitment, which will sustain you through two years of service. Pre-service training can be a stressful and challenging time, but you will find a great deal of support from an experienced training staff. Training is intensive (24 hours a day, 7 days a week). Weekends are considered an essential part of the community integration experience. Therefore, you will only be permitted two nights out of your training community during PST. These nights are to be taken separately, beginning after the first month of training. Vacation is not permitted during PST or during your first three months of service. Trainees are not allowed to receive international visitors during PST.

Additional Trainings During Volunteer Service

In its commitment to institutionalize quality training, the Peace Corps has implemented a training system that provides Volunteers with continual opportunities to examine their commitment to Peace Corps service while increasing their technical and cross-cultural skills. During service, there are usually three training events. The titles and objectives for those trainings are as follows:

- In-service training: *Provides an opportunity for Volunteers to upgrade their technical, language, and project development skills while sharing their experiences and reaffirming their commitment after having served for three months.*

- Midterm conference: *Assists Volunteers in reviewing their first year, reassessing their personal and project objectives, and planning for their second year of service.*

- Close-of-service conference: *Prepares Volunteers for the future after Peace Corps service and reviews their respective projects and personal experiences.*

The number, length, and design of these trainings are adapted to country-specific needs and conditions. The key to the training system is that training events are integrated and interrelated, from the pre-departure orientation through the end of your service, and are planned, implemented, and evaluated cooperatively by the training staff, Peace Corps staff, and Volunteers.

YOUR HEALTH CARE AND SAFETY IN COSTA RICA

The Peace Corps' highest priority is maintaining the good health and safety of every Volunteer. Peace Corps medical programs emphasize the preventive, rather than the curative, approach to disease. The Peace Corps in Costa Rica maintains a clinic with a full-time medical officer, who takes care of Volunteers' primary health-care needs. Additional medical services, such as testing and basic treatment, are also available in Costa Rica at local hospitals. If you become seriously ill, you will be transported either to an American-standard medical facility in the region or to the United States.

Health Issues in Costa Rica

Health conditions in Costa Rica are typical of those found in tropical countries. Most illnesses can be avoided by using common sense and following basic preventive measures. Because you may be serving in areas where malaria, a mosquito-borne disease, is prevalent, you may be provided with and required to take an approved anti-malarial drug during the entire 27 months of service. Or, if you live outside malaria-infected areas and plan to visit them, you will be expected to take the provided medication as instructed by medical staff, including during trips out of the country. Failure to comply with Peace Corps' regulations regarding malaria medication is grounds for separation from the Peace Corps.

Humidity and heat promote the growth of skin infections, which you can help prevent by keeping your body clean and dry as much as possible. Environmental pollution, mold, and pollen found throughout the country year-round can aggravate existing environmental allergies. The Peace Corps does not provide allergy testing. Other illnesses that exist in Costa Rica are dengue fever, rabies, tuberculosis, intestinal parasites, hepatitis A and B, and sexually transmitted infections (STIs), including HIV/AIDS, among others.

Helping You Stay Healthy

The Peace Corps will provide you with all the necessary inoculations, medications, and information to stay healthy. Upon your arrival in Costa Rica, you will receive a medical handbook. At the end of training, you will receive a medical kit with supplies to take care of mild illnesses and first aid needs. The contents of the kit are listed later in this section.

During pre-service training, you will have access to basic medical supplies through the medical officer. However, during this time, you will be responsible for your own supply of prescription drugs and any other specific medical supplies you require, as the Peace Corps will not order these items during training. Please bring a three-month supply of any prescription drugs you use, since they may not be available here and it may take several months for shipments to arrive.

You will have physicals at midservice and at the end of your service. If you develop a serious medical problem during your service, the medical officer in Costa Rica will consult with the Office of Medical Services in Washington, D.C. If it is determined that your condition cannot be treated in Costa Rica, you may be sent out of the country for further evaluation and care.

Maintaining Your Health

As a Volunteer, you must accept considerable responsibility for your own health. Proper precautions will significantly reduce your risk of serious illness or injury. The adage "An ounce of prevention is worth a pound of cure" becomes extremely important in areas where diagnostic and treatment facilities are not up to the standards of the United States. The most important of your responsibilities in Costa Rica is to take the following preventive measures:

- Boiling or treating drinking water

- Washing fruits and vegetables with soap and water
- Receiving and taking the necessary prophylaxis

By following these preventive measures you will minimize your chances of contracting food poisoning, parasitic infections, hepatitis A, dysentery, tapeworms, and typhoid fever. Your medical officer will discuss specific standards for water and food preparation in Costa Rica during pre-service training.

Abstinence is the most effective way to prevent infection with HIV and other STIs. You are taking risks if you choose to be sexually active. To lessen risk, use a condom every time you have sex. Whether your partner is a host country national, a fellow Volunteer, or anyone else, do not assume or take his or her word that this person is free of HIV/AIDS or other STIs.

Volunteers who are sexually activeare expected to adhere to an effective means of birth control to prevent an unplanned pregnancy. Your medical officer can help you decide on the most appropriate method to suit your individual needs. Certain (but not all) contraceptive methods are available without charge from the medical office.

A male Peace Corps Volunteer who fathers a child out of wedlock may be administratively separated if the country director determines that the Volunteer's action has impaired his ability to perform his assignment or has violated local laws or customs. The Peace Corps will pay the prenatal, delivery, and postpartum costs for a non-Volunteer spouse or unmarried partner only if the Volunteer has taken action to acknowledge paternity of the child and only for costs incurred while the trainee or Volunteer is in service. Paternity legislation in Costa Rica states that DNA testing is mandatory when a woman claims a man is the father of her child. If the test establishes paternity, the father automatically must pay child support; if he does not comply, he can be jailed.

It is critical to your health that you promptly report to the medical office for scheduled immunizations, and that you let the medical officers know immediately of significant illnesses and injuries.

Women's Health Information

Pregnancy is treated in the same manner as other Volunteer health conditions that require medical attention but also have programmatic ramifications. The Peace Corps is responsible for determining the medical risk and the availability of appropriate medical care if the Volunteer remains in-country. Given the circumstances under which Volunteers live and work in Peace Corps countries, it is rare that the Peace Corps' medical and programmatic standards for continued service during pregnancy can be met.

If feminine hygiene products are not available for you to purchase on the local market, the Peace Corps medical officer in Costa Rica will provide them. If you require a specific product, please bring a three-month supply with you.

Your Peace Corps Medical Kit

The Peace Corps medical officer will provide you with a kit that contains basic items necessary to prevent and treat illnesses that may occur during service. Kit items can be periodically restocked at the medical office.

Medical Kit Contents

Ace bandages

Adhesive tape

American Red Cross First Aid & Safety Handbook

Antacid tablets (Tums)

Antibiotic ointment (Bacitracin/Neomycin/Polymycin B)

Antiseptic antimicrobial skin cleaner (Hibiclens)

Band-Aids

Butterfly closures

Calamine lotion

Cepacol lozenges

Condoms

Dental floss

Diphenhydramine HCL 25 mg (Benadryl)

Insect repellent stick (Cutter)

Iodine tablets (for water purification)

Lip balm (Chapstick)

Oral rehydration salts

Oral thermometer (Fahrenheit)

Pseudoephedrine HCL 30 mg (Sudafed)

Robitussin-DM lozenges (for cough)

Scissors

Sterile gauze pads

Tetrahydrozaline eyedrops (Visine)

Tinactin (antifungal cream)

Tweezers

Before You Leave: A Medical Checklist

If there has been any change in your health—physical, mental, or dental—since you submitted your examination reports to the Peace Corps, you must immediately notify the Office of Medical Services. Failure to disclose new illnesses, injuries, allergies, or pregnancy can endanger your health and may jeopardize your eligibility to serve.

If your dental exam was done more than a year ago, or if your physical exam is more than two years old, contact the Office of Medical Services to find out whether you need to update your records. If your dentist or Peace Corps dental consultant has recommended that you undergo dental treatment or repair, you must complete that work and make sure your dentist sends requested confirmation reports or X-rays to the Office of Medical Services.

If you wish to avoid having duplicate vaccinations, contact your physician's office to obtain a copy of your immunization record and bring it to your pre-departure orientation. If you have any immunizations prior to Peace Corps service, the Peace Corps cannot reimburse you for the cost. The Peace Corps will provide all the immunizations necessary for your overseas assignment, either at your pre-departure orientation or shortly after you arrive in Costa Rica. You do not need to begin taking malaria medication prior to departure.

Bring a three-month supply of any prescription or over-the-counter medication you use on a regular basis, including birth control pills. Although the Peace Corps cannot reimburse you for this three-month supply, it will order refills during your service. While awaiting shipment—which can take several months—you will be dependent on your own medication supply. The Peace Corps will not pay for herbal or nonprescribed medications, such as St. John's wort, glucosamine, selenium, or antioxidant supplements.

You are encouraged to bring copies of medical prescriptions signed by your physician. This is not a requirement, but they might come in handy if you are questioned in transit about carrying a three-month supply of prescription drugs.

If you wear eyeglasses, bring two pairs with you. If a pair breaks, the Peace Corps will replace them, using the information your doctor in the United States provided on the eyeglasses form during your examination. The Peace Corps discourages you from using contact lenses during your service to reduce your risk of developing a serious infection or other eye disease. Most Peace Corps countries do not have appropriate water and sanitation to support eye care with the use of contact lenses. The Peace Corps will not supply or replace contact lenses or associated solutions unless an ophthalmologist has recommended their use for a specific medical condition and the Peace Corps Office of Medical Services has given approval.

If you are eligible for Medicare, are over 50 years of age, or have a health condition that may restrict your future participation in health-care plans, you may wish to consult an insurance specialist about unique coverage needs before your departure. The Peace Corps will provide all necessary health care from the time you leave for your pre-departure orientation until you complete your service. When you finish, you will be entitled to the post-service health-care benefits described in the Peace Corps Volunteer Handbook. You may wish to consider keeping an existing health plan in effect during your service if you think age or pre-existing conditions might prevent you from re-enrolling in your current plan when you return home.

Safety and Security—Our Partnership

Serving as a Volunteer overseas entails certain safety and security risks. Living and traveling in an unfamiliar environment, a limited understanding of the local language and culture, and the perception of being a wealthy American are some of the factors that can put a Volunteer at risk. Property theft and burglaries are not uncommon. Incidents of physical and sexual assault do occur, although almost all Volunteers complete their two years of service without serious personal safety problems.

Beyond knowing that Peace Corps approaches safety and security as a partnership with you, it might be helpful to see how this partnership works. Peace Corps has policies, procedures, and training in place to promote your safety. The Peace Corps depends on you to follow those policies and to put into practice what you have learned. An example of how this works in practice—in this case to help manage the risk of burglary—is as follows:

- Peace Corps assesses the security environment where you will live and work
- Peace Corps inspects the house where you will live according to established security criteria
- Peace Corps provides you with resources to take measures such as installing new locks
- Peace Corps ensures you are welcomed by host country authorities in your new community
- Peace Corps responds to security concerns that you raise
- You lock your doors and windows
- You adopt a lifestyle appropriate to the community where you live
- You get to know neighbors
- You decide if purchasing personal articles insurance is appropriate for you
- You don't change residences before being authorized by Peace Corps
- You communicate concerns that you have to Peace Corps staff

This welcome book contains sections on Living Conditions and Volunteer Lifestyle, Peace Corps Training, and Your Health Care and Safety that all include important safety and security information to help you understand this partnership. The Peace Corps makes every effort to give Volunteers the tools they need to function in the safest way possible, because working to maximize the safety and security of Volunteers is our highest priority. Not only do we provide you with training and tools to prepare for the unexpected, but we teach you to identify, reduce, and manage the risks you may encounter.

Factors that Contribute to Volunteer Risk

There are several factors that can heighten a Volunteer's risk, many of which are within the Volunteer's control. By far the most common crime that Volunteers experience is theft. Thefts often occur when Volunteers are away from their sites, in crowded locations (such as markets or on public transportation), and when leaving items unattended.

Before you depart for Costa Rica there are several measures you can take to reduce your risk:

- Leave valuable objects in U.S.
- Leave copies of important documents and account numbers with someone you trust in the U.S.
- Purchase a hidden money pouch or "dummy" wallet as a decoy
- Purchase personal articles insurance

After you arrive in Costa Rica, you will receive more detailed information about common crimes, factors that contribute to Volunteer risk, and local strategies to reduce that risk. For example, Volunteers in Costa Rica learn to do the following:

- Choose safe routes and times for travel, and travel with someone trusted by the community whenever possible
- Make sure one's personal appearance is respectful of local customs
- Avoid high-crime areas
- Know the local language to get help in an emergency
- Make friends with local people who are respected in the community
- Limit alcohol consumption

As you can see from this list, you must be willing to work hard and adapt your lifestyle to minimize the potential for being a target for crime. As with anywhere in the world, crime occurs in Costa Rica. You can reduce your risk by avoiding situations that place you at risk and by taking precautions. Crime at the village or town level is less frequent than in the large cities; people know each other and generally are less likely to steal from their neighbors. Tourist attractions in large towns are favorite worksites for pickpockets.

The following are other security concerns in Costa Rica of which you should be aware:

The U.S. Department of State currently considers the crime rate in Costa Rica high. While common criminal activity is similar to what is found in any large U.S. city, there are criminal activities that are particular to Costa Rica. Criminals frequently prey on tourists through street scams, ATM thefts, and robbery on public buses. Credit card fraud or numbers skimming is common. Numbers skimming is the theft of the information contained in the magnetic strip on the backside of the credit card. The theft of the information occurs when a criminal swipes the card through a machine that stores all the information. With this information the criminal can charge items to the unsuspecting victim's credit card. Only when the monthly invoice arrives does the victim realize that he or she has been swindled. Volunteers who choose to use their credit cards should carefully monitor their records and frequently check their credit card accounts. Volunteers should avoid use of debit cards for point-of-sale purchases.

Political Violence

Costa Rica has the longest history of democracy in Central America. Indigenous terrorist organizations are nonexistent. There is no known organization targeting U.S. citizens or U.S.-affiliated interests in Costa Rica. Labor strikes and protests are common in Costa Rica. While normally peaceful, all protests and demonstrations should be avoided.

Natural Disasters

Costa Rica lies within an active earthquake zone, and periodically experiences significant tremors. The last earthquaketo cause significant damage to Costa Rica's infrastructure occurred in January 2009 near San José and measured 6.2 on the Richter scale. In late 2004, an earthquake registered 6.2, and in December 2005, another earthquake registered 5.1. Costa Rica is also a micro-climate, and Volunteers who wish to travel should check the projected rainfall amounts for the area in Costa Rica they intend to visit. Flooding may occur around the port city of Limon or other lower-elevation areas of Costa Rica at any time, regardless of time of year and projected rainfall amount in a particular region.

Transportation Safety

Costa Rica has one of the highest vehicle accident rates in the world. Poor road conditions and erratic driving are daily hazards in Costa Rica. Roads outside of San Jose are generally in poor condition. The roads are often overcrowded and narrow; drivers should be on the lookout for large potholes, road washouts, and mudslides during the rainy season (May through November). Speed limits and red lights are often ignored. It is very common for vehicles to cross multiple lanes of traffic without regard to other drivers. Pedestrians are not given the right of way, and extreme caution should be used whenever walking on the streets. Motorcycles are prevalent on the road and weave through traffic in any type of traffic situation.

Passport Theft

Costa Rica's immigration service conducts random inspections throughout the country. Travelers should be prepared to present their passports upon entry into Costa Rica. Due to a recent change in Costa Rican immigration regulations, photocopies of passports depicting the biographical and entry stamp pages can be carried while in Costa Rica.

Criminals looking to illegally enter the United States may target U.S. passports for theft. The U.S. Embassy reports that Costa Rica is the world's single largest offender of lost or stolen U.S. passports. Passports have been reported stolen from inside the airport, as well as other locations throughout Costa Rica.

While whistles and exclamations may be fairly common on the street, this behavior can be reduced if you dress conservatively, abide by local cultural norms, and respond according to the training you will receive.

Staying Safe: Don't Be a Target for Crime

You must be prepared to take on a large degree of responsibility for your own safety. You can make yourself less of a target, ensure that your home is secure, and develop relationships in your community that will make you an unlikely victim of crime. While the factors that contribute to your risk in Costa Rica may be different, in many ways you can do what you would do if you moved to a new city anywhere: Be cautious, check things out, ask questions, learn about your neighborhood, know where the more risky locations are, use common sense, and be aware. You can reduce your vulnerability to crime by integrating into your community, learning the local language, acting responsibly, and abiding by Peace Corps policies and procedures. Serving safely and effectively in Costa Rica will require that you accept some restrictions on your current lifestyle.

Support from Staff

If a trainee or Volunteer is the victim of a safety incident, Peace Corps staff is prepared to provide support. All Peace Corps posts have procedures in place to respond to incidents of crime committed against Volunteers. The first priority for all posts in the aftermath of an incident is to ensure the Volunteer is safe and receiving medical treatment as needed. After assuring the safety of the Volunteer, Peace Corps staff response may include reassessing the Volunteer's worksite and housing arrangements and making any adjustments, as needed. In some cases, the nature of the incident may necessitate a site or housing transfer. Peace Corps staff will also assist Volunteers with preserving their rights to pursue legal sanctions against the perpetrators of the crime. It is very important that Volunteers report incidents as they occur, not only to protect their peer Volunteers, but also to preserve the future right to prosecute. Should Volunteers decide later in the process that they want to proceed with the prosecution of their assailant, this option may no longer exist if the evidence of the event has not been preserved at the time of the incident.

Crime Data for Costa Rica

Crime data and statistics for Costa Rica, which are updated yearly, are available at the following link: http://www.peacecorps.gov/countrydata/costarica

Please take the time to review this important information.

Few Peace Corps Volunteers are victims of serious crimes and crimes that do occur overseas are investigated and prosecuted by local authorities through the local courts system. If you are the victim of a crime, you will decide if you wish to pursue prosecution. If you decide to prosecute, the Peace Corps will be there to assist you. One of our tasks is to ensure you are fully informed of your options and understand how the local legal process works. The Peace Corps will help you ensure your rights are protected to the fullest extent possible under the laws of the country.

If you are the victim of a serious crime, you will learn how to get to a safe location as quickly as possible and contact your Peace Corps office. It's important that you notify Peace Corps staff as soon as you can so the Peace Corps can provide you with the help you need.

Volunteer Safety Support in Costa Rica

The Peace Corps' approach to safety is a five-pronged plan to help you stay safe during your service and includes the following: information sharing, Volunteer training, site selection criteria, a detailed emergency action plan, and protocols for addressing safety and security incidents. Costa Rica's in-country safety program is outlined below.

The Peace Corps/Costa Rica office will keep you informed of any issues that may impact Volunteer safety through **information sharing**. Regular updates will be provided in Volunteer newsletters and in memorandums from the country director. In the event of a critical situation or emergency, you will be contacted through the emergency communication network. An important component of the capacity of Peace Corps to keep you informed is your buy-in to the partnership concept with the Peace Corps staff. It is expected that you will do your part in ensuring that Peace Corps staff members are kept apprised of your movements in-country so they are able to inform you.

Volunteer training will include sessions on specific safety and security issues in Costa Rica. This training will prepare you to adopt a culturally appropriate lifestyle and exercise judgment that promotes safety and reduces risk in your home, at work, and while traveling. Safety training is offered throughout service and is integrated into the language, cross-cultural aspects, health, and other components of training. You will be expected to successfully complete all training competencies in a variety of areas, including safety and security, as a condition of service.

Certain **site selection criteria** are used to determine safe housing for Volunteers before their arrival. The Peace Corps staff works closely with host communities and partner agencies to help prepare them for a Volunteer's arrival and to establish expectations of their respective roles in supporting the Volunteer. Each site is inspected before the Volunteer's arrival to ensure placement in appropriate, safe, and secure housing and worksites. Site selection is based, in part, on any relevant site history; access to medical, banking, postal, and other essential services; availability of communications, transportation, and markets; different housing options and living arrangements; and other Volunteer support needs.

You will also learn about Peace Corps/Costa Rica's **detailed emergency action plan,** which is implemented in the event of civil or political unrest or a natural disaster. When you arrive at your site, you will complete and submit a site locator form with your address, contact information, and a map to your house. If there is a security threat, you will gather with other Volunteers in Costa Rica at predetermined locations until the situation is resolved or the Peace Corps decides to evacuate.

Finally, in order for the Peace Corps to be fully responsive to the needs of Volunteers, it is imperative that Volunteers immediately report any security incident to the Peace Corps office. The Peace Corps has established **protocols for addressing safety and security incidents** in a timely and appropriate manner, and it collects and evaluates safety and security data to track trends and develop strategies to minimize risks to future Volunteers.

DIVERSITY AND CROSS-CULTURAL ISSUES

In fulfilling its mandate to share the face of America with host countries, the Peace Corps is making special efforts to assure that all of America's richness is reflected in the Volunteer corps. More Americans of color are serving in today's Peace Corps than at any time in recent history. Differences in race, ethnic background, age, religion, and sexual orientation are expected and welcomed among Volunteers. Part of the Peace Corps mission is to help dispel any notion that Americans are all of one origin or race and to establish that each of us is as thoroughly American as the other despite our many differences.

Diversity helps the Peace Corps accomplish that goal. In other ways, however, it poses challenges. In Costa Rica, as in other Peace Corps host countries, Volunteers' behavior, lifestyle, background, and beliefs are judged in a cultural context very different from their own. Certain personal perspectives or characteristics commonly accepted in the United States may be quite uncommon, unacceptable, or even repressed in Costa Rica.

Outside of Costa Rica's capital, residents of rural communities have had relatively little direct exposure to other cultures, races, religions, and lifestyles. What people view as typical American behavior or norms may be a misconception, such as the belief that all Americans are rich and have blond hair and blue eyes. The people of Costa Rica are justly known for their generous hospitality to foreigners; however, members of the community in which you will live may display a range of reactions to cultural differences that you present.

To ease the transition and adapt to life in Costa Rica, you may need to make some temporary, yet fundamental compromises in how you present yourself as an American and as an individual. For example, female trainees and Volunteers may not be able to exercise the independence available to them in the United States, political discussions need to be handled with great care, and some of your personal beliefs may best remain undisclosed. You will need to develop techniques and personal strategies for coping with these and other limitations. The Peace Corps staff will lead diversity and sensitivity discussions during pre-service training and will be on call to provide support, but the challenge ultimately will be your own.

Overview of Diversity in Costa Rica

The Peace Corps staff in Costa Rica recognizes the adjustment issues that come with diversity and will endeavor to provide support and guidance. During pre-service training, several sessions will be held to discuss diversity and coping mechanisms. Peace Corps/Costa Rica looks forward to having male and female Volunteers from a variety of races, ethnic groups, ages, religions, and sexual orientations, and hope that you will become part of a diverse group of Americans who take pride in supporting one another and demonstrating the richness of American culture.

What Might a Volunteer Face?

Possible Issues for Female Volunteers

As in all Latin American countries, Costa Rican society can be considered *machista* and Volunteers, especially women, are often bothered by the machismo aspect of Costa Rican culture. Some men hiss or make amorous and sexually suggestive comments to any woman (foreigner or local) who walks by, which can be frustrating. Many female Volunteers deal with this issue by completely ignoring the comments; others continue to be bothered by them for their entire two years of service. In the workplace, it can be difficult to know when a comment is culturally acceptable and when it constitutes harassment. It is safe to say that most women never accept the catcalls and sexual harassment; rather, they develop a degree of tolerance with which they can function effectively.

Female Volunteers may also experience discomfort with seeing females assume primary responsibility for household chores (i.e., child care, cleaning, and cooking). In addition, many female Volunteers find it difficult to maintain friendships with Costa Rican males because of the assumption that there is always a sexual element to any male-female relationship. Many ticos' (Costa Rican natives) impressions of American females come from American media, such as "Sex and the City," "90210," and other TV series that portray promiscuity. A female Volunteer may feel it appropriate and platonic to invite a male tico friend into her home, but most ticos will interpret this as an invitation for intimacy.

Depending on the norms at one's site, female Volunteers may not be able to exercise the freedoms to which North American women are accustomed. While some Costa Rican women occupy top government positions, traditional roles for women prevail outside of the capital city and its surroundings. This is a source of frustration for some female Volunteers.

Possible Issues for Male Volunteers

Male Volunteers also must deal with the machismo of the society. Men may be expected to show their machismo by making sexual comments and by not fulfilling household activities (such as washing the dishes and doing the laundry). Many Costa Rican mothers consider an American male to be a great catch for their daughters. Although male Volunteers may not be bothered by these perceptions, they can interfere with relationships and work in the community.

Possible Issues for Volunteers of Color

The majority of the tourists who visit Costa Rica are white. Consequently, host country nationals tend to think that all North Americans are white, and they sometimes mistake non-Caucasian Volunteers for being from somewhere other than the United States. For instance, African Americans or Hispanic Americans may be thought to be from Costa Rica or other Latin American countries. Similarly, Volunteers of Asian descent are often considered Chinese regardless of their family's country of origin.

Volunteers of color have different reactions to this situation, depending on their perceptions and circumstances. For example, a light-skinned African American blended into Costa Rican culture without any problems and found this to be helpful when buying goods at the market. People assumed that she was a local resident, not an American, so she was not charged inflated prices. However, another Volunteer with much darker skin was frustrated by the prejudice against people with darker skin in some areas of the country.

African-American Volunteers may be assumed to be from the Caribbean area of the country and ascribed attributes of that subculture. They may be called negro (black), the local word commonly used to describe black people, whether used in a derogatory way or as a term of endearment. They may be one of the few minority members in the program and they may work and live with individuals who have no understanding of African-American cultures.

Hispanic-American Volunteers may not be perceived as being North American. They may be expected to speak Spanish fluently because of a Hispanic surname. Costa Ricans may assume that Hispanic Americans understand the culture and language and, thus, expect them to interact socially with more ease.

Asian-American Volunteers may be identified by their ethnic heritage, not by their American citizenship. They may be perceived in a certain way based on Costa Rica's current or historical involvement with Asian countries (especially China) or the increased presence of Asian businessmen in the community as bar, restaurant, and shop owners.

Volunteer Comment:
"Little by little, you have to start educating people and be prepared to face racist comments, which are always popping up. You need to be tolerant and take the initiative to educate others."

Possible Issues for Senior Volunteers

More than younger Volunteers, older Volunteers may have challenges in maintaining lifelong friendships and dealing with financial matters from afar. They may want to consider assigning power of attorney to someone.

A senior may be the only older person in a group of Volunteers and initially may not feel part of the group. Younger Volunteers may look to an older Volunteer for advice and support; some seniors find this to be an enjoyable experience, while others choose not to fill this role. Some seniors may find it difficult to adapt to a lack of structure and clarity in their role after having worked for many years in a very structured and demanding job.

Some senior trainees find the intensity of training quite tiring. Others experience a lack of attention to their particular language learning needs and may need to be assertive in developing an effective individual approach.

Volunteer Comment:
"Because of the level of development in Costa Rica, I didn't find that my age impeded or made my service more difficult. In fact, people in Costa Rica are very open to and respectful of older people."

Possible Issues for Gay, Lesbian, or Bisexual Volunteers

Although homosexuality is present in Costa Rica, it is not yet accepted in many parts of the country and there is still a great deal of prejudice toward homosexuals. Few gay, lesbian, or bisexual Volunteers choose to be open about their sexual orientation during service. Just as many Volunteers do not share every aspect of their personality with their communities, some Volunteers wait until they are well integrated before choosing to disclose their sexual orientation to prevent risking work and personal relationships. Volunteers who do come out have to deal with questions about boy/girlfriends, marriage, and sex (as do all Volunteers). There are local gay, lesbian, bisexual, and transgender organizations, which are a "safe space" for Volunteers to network and seek support.

Possible Religious Issues for Volunteers

Costa Rica is a largely Roman Catholic country and the church plays an important role in the political debate of the country and in the society's moral beliefs. There is no separation of church and state as it exists in the United States. Some Costa Ricans you meet may not know much, or may have misconceptions, about other religions. However, there are congregations of other religions in Costa Rica (e.g., Baptist, Methodist, Jewish, Lutheran, Anglican, Mormon, Jehovah's Witnesses, etc.).

Volunteer Comment:
"Due to the fact that there is a strong presence of the Roman Catholic Church, other religions and denominations can be looked down upon."

Possible Issues for Volunteers With Disabilities

As part of the medical clearance process, the Peace Corps Office of Medical Services determined that you were physically and emotionally capable, with or without reasonable accommodations, to perform a full tour of Volunteer service in Costa Rica without unreasonable risk of harm to yourself or interruption of service. The Peace Corps/Costa Rica staff will work with Volunteers with disabilities to make reasonable accommodations for them in training, housing, jobsites, or other areas to enable them to serve safely and effectively.

The infrastructure in Costa Rica does not make many accommodations for people with physical disabilities. Volunteers' primary mode of transportation is on foot and public transportation. Public buses in Costa Rica are not equipped to accommodate people with physical disabilities; getting on and off the bus requires being able to step up or down 1-2 feet. Most communities do not have sidewalks, and very few have ramps. Rural communities generally have uneven, unpaved roads that are susceptible to flooding, potholes, and muddy conditions that may inhibit mobility, particularly during the rainy season. In addition, Costa Ricans sometimes give nicknames to people based on their physical characteristics, including disabilities, and you may experience prejudice or jokes about your disability. Depending on your disability, there may be few local resources to turn to for support.

Possible Issues for Married Volunteers

Married PCV couples are faced with unique challenges and experiences. Serving in such a family-oriented country, you may be asked certain questions, such as: Do you have children? Why don't you have any children? When do you plan on having children? Why haven't you had any children yet? Another challenge you may face as a couple is following the roles a husband and wife have in Costa Rica. In some households husbands work away from the home and provide for their families, while wives stay home to cook, clean, and care for the children. Although this situation is changing with women working out of the house, a woman is still expected to care for her husband. As a wife, you may be asked about food, laundry, and other household decisions. It is not uncommon that you, as a wife, may be expected to serve your husband food. Men may be subject to some light teasing from community members if they are seen cooking or cleaning.

FREQUENTLY ASKED QUESTIONS

How much luggage am I allowed to bring to Costa Rica?

Most airlines have baggage size and weight limits and assess charges for transport of baggage that exceeds those limits. The Peace Corps has its own size and weight limits and will not pay the cost of transport for baggage that exceeds these limits. The Peace Corps' allowance is two checked pieces of luggage with combined dimensions of both pieces not to exceed 107 inches (length + width + height) and a carry-on bag with dimensions of no more than 45 inches. Checked baggage should not exceed 100 pounds total with a maximum weight of 50 pounds for any one bag.

Peace Corps Volunteers are not allowed to take pets, weapons, explosives, radio transmitters (shortwave radios are permitted), automobiles, or motorcycles to their overseas assignments. Do not pack flammable materials or liquids such as lighter fluid, cleaning solvents, hair spray, or aerosol containers. This is an important safety precaution.

What is the electric current in Costa Rica?

The electric current generally is 110 volts, as in the United States; however, there are 220-volt outlets for some appliances (e.g., refrigerators and electric ovens).

How much money should I bring?

Volunteers are expected to live at the same level as the people in their community. You will be given a settling-in allowance and a monthly living allowance, which should cover your expenses. Volunteers often wish to bring additional money for vacation travel to other countries. Credit cards and traveler's checks are preferable to cash. If you choose to bring extra money, bring the amount that will suit your own travel plans and needs.

When can I take vacation and have people visit me?

Each Volunteer accrues two vacation days per month of service (excluding training). Leave may not be taken during training, the first three months of service, or the last three months of service, except in conjunction with an authorized emergency leave. Family and friends are welcome to visit you after pre-service training and the first three months of service as long as their stay does not interfere with your work. Extended stays at your site are not encouraged and may require permission from your country director. The Peace Corps is not able to provide your visitors with visa, medical, or travel assistance.

Will my belongings be covered by insurance?

The Peace Corps does not provide insurance coverage for personal effects; Volunteers are ultimately responsible for the safekeeping of their personal belongings. However, you can purchase personal property insurance before you leave. If you wish, you may contact your own insurance company; additionally, insurance application forms will be provided, and you are encouraged to consider them carefully. Volunteers should not ship or take valuable items overseas. Jewelry, watches, radios, cameras, and expensive appliances are subject to loss, theft, and breakage, and in many places, satisfactory maintenance and repair services are not available.

Do I need an international driver's license?

Volunteers in Costa Rica do not need an international driver's license because they are prohibited from operating privately owned motorized vehicles, except while on authorized vacation. If on vacation, a Volunteer must secure a Costa Rican driver's license. Most urban travel is by bus or taxi. Rural travel ranges from buses and minibuses to trucks, bicycles, and lots of walking.

What should I bring as gifts for Costa Rica friends and my host family?

This is not a requirement. A token of friendship is sufficient. Some gift suggestions include knickknacks for the house; pictures, books, or calendars of American scenes; souvenirs from your area; hard candies that will not melt or spoil; or photos to give away.

Where will my site assignment be when I finish training and how isolated will I be?

Peace Corps trainees are not assigned to individual sites until after they have completed pre-service training. This gives Peace Corps staff the opportunity to assess each trainee's technical and language skills prior to assigning sites, in addition to finalizing site selections with their ministry partners. If feasible, you may have the opportunity to provide input on your site preferences, including geographical location, distance from other Volunteers, and living conditions. However, keep in mind that many factors influence the site selection process and that the Peace Corps cannot guarantee placement where you would ideally like to be. Most Volunteers live in small towns or in rural villages and are usually within one hour from another Volunteer. Sites range from - two- to 10-hour drive from the capital.

How can my family contact me in an emergency?

The Peace Corps Counseling and Outreach Unit (COU) provides assistance in handling emergencies affecting trainees and Volunteers or their families. Before leaving the United States, instruct your family to notify COU immediately if an emergency arises, such as a serious illness or death of a family member. During normal business hours, the number for COU is 855.855.1961; select option 2, then extension 1470. After normal business hours and on weekends and holidays, the COU duty officer can be reached at the above number. For non-emergency questions, your family can get information from your country desk staff at the Peace Corps by calling 855.855.1961.

Can I call home from Costa Rica?

Yes, you can call home from any public or private phone, collect or with a calling card. There are international operators for Sprint, AT&T, and MCI. In addition, you can purchase international calling cards issued by the national telephone company at many stores throughout Costa Rica. Many Volunteers now use Skype from personal computers or Internet cafes to make inexpensive international phone calls.

Should I bring a cellular phone with me?

The Peace Corps discourages you from bringing a cellular phone because it may not be compatible with the technology in Costa Rica. In the past year, some Volunteers have been able to activate unblocked cellphones purchased in the U.S. There is an open and competitive cellphone industry in Costa Rica, making more options available to Volunteers for the purchase of cellphones and cell service. Public phones are readily available, and most host families have landline telephones. If you choose to bring a cellular phone with you, you must bring the receipt. The phone company will review the receipt to ensure the phone was not stolen.

Will there be email and Internet access?

There are Internet services in many communities. However, Volunteers assigned to rural sites or small towns may have to travel by bus to the nearest commercial center to access email and the Internet. Some Volunteers have limited access to computers in the local office of their national host country partner agencies.

Should I bring my computer?

You do not need to bring a personal computer to Costa Rica, but Volunteers who choose to bring laptops are generally satisfied with their decision, as access to a computer facilitates work, enables communication, and enhances entertainment options. Should you choose to bring a laptop, it will be your responsibility to maintain and insure it; the Peace Corps will not be responsible for any damage or theft.

WELCOME LETTERS FROM COSTA RICA VOLUNTEERS

Dear Future Peace Corps/Costa Rica Trainee,

Congratulations! It is no small feat to endure the arduous application process and to arrive at the threshold of your Peace Corps experience. In development work, every step forward and every goal achieved is an important success. These are exciting times. While you may be frantically pondering the things you'll need to bring or the jobs you'll be leaving behind, *tranquilo.* I hope you find a moment to properly celebrate this accomplishment.

I would also like to extol your decision to be a Peace Corps Volunteer. The very idea of this type of volunteerism is radical and your persistence to continue on this path belies an understanding that truthful exchange in the pursuit of promoting peace and recognizing our basic human connection often demands sacrifice. Leaving the ones we cherish and a world with known quantities is never easy. For perhaps the first time in your life, you will be separated from your family and friends not only by time and distance, but by a large gaping difference in daily cultural experience. Routines and plans will change and other professional or scholarly opportunities will be delayed or left behind. But many apply, few are invited, and fewer still decide to take the plunge. Perhaps you even have family members or friends who once considered Peace Corps. Take pride in the knowledge that you not only were invited, but decided to heed that adventurous part of your being. And although your life will be placed on hold for the next two years, know that many more opportunities await you at the end of your service.

But what does it mean to be a Peace Corps Volunteer in Costa Rica, much less a Volunteer in the Youth in Development project? At its best, Costa Rica is an example to nations everywhere that another world, a peaceful world, is possible. Broadly speaking then, our goal is not only to promote peace in Costa Rica, but to maintain it. We accomplish this through the practice of a grassroots, participatory-based methodology that brings you face-to-face with the community. Problems and solutions are generated from the people and as Volunteers, we act as facilitators and guides, community advocates and assets, and less definably so, as creative sparks that attempt to change the narrative many communities wish to change, but fail to see beyond. As a youth development Volunteer, you'll be expected to teach life skills to youth, and to some extent adults, and to build relationships with existing institutions and organizations on the national and local levels to develop and implement sustainable solutions.

Because we live in the communities with which we work, Peace Corps service truly is a 24-hour job. It is life in its dullest and fullest forms. It is strife with tedium, contradiction, and failure as much as euphoric breakthroughs and surprises. You will experience everything from loneliness to suffocation by attention. It is as much a time for introspection and reflection as it is for action. Plans you make can quickly fall apart, discouragingly and frequently so. Though Costa Rica has a reputation of being a "cushy placement" by Peace Corps standards, it is far from a universal truth. In many ways, volunteer work in Costa Rica is more difficult, as the seeming abundance of resources and vestiges of modern development provoke a sort of cognitive dissonance. There are many avenues for social improvement, but accessibility greatly varies, as does their actual use by relevant populations. Costa Rica is beautiful and full of potential, but it still is a developing country.

However, if you keep yourself calm and open, and manage to navigate the peaks and valleys of this experience, wonderful things happen. The possibilities dot the spectrum: *cafecito* with a community member, meetings with officials and local organizations, soccer and other impromptu games in the plaza, random lessons about English and culture, honest discussion about social issues, jaunts to farms or into the surrounding natural environment, cooking lessons about the local fare, and countless more. At the heart of these activities is the forging of connections. If nothing else, the bonds you form with your community and your fellow Volunteers will provide strength for the hard times and lasting memories of a lifetime. And like any given relationship, building trust and transforming momentum into positive change is slow. Development work is slow. Be patient. Be ready. The "Peace Corps Experience" is a departure from what we've known, but it is only a beginning. You'll arrive with the desire to move mountains, but be flexible and willing to start small. You've been invited to undertake this challenge. We think you're ready and we're excited to have you. Welcome to Peace Corps/Costa Rica. *Pura Vida.*

Sincerely,

Allen Sin
Tico 22
Youth in Development Project

***

Dear Future CED Volunteer,

Congratulations! You have been chosen for one of the Peace Corps' most vibrant posts—where it has served uninterrupted since 1963 and Volunteers report high levels of satisfaction. You'll find plenty of excitement— and work to be done—in Costa Rica.

When I was in your shoes, I stayed up late reading everything I could find about Peace Corps/Costa Rica. You probably feel excited, overwhelmed, and in the dark about what awaits you. Don't worry. No matter how little you pack or how little you know, you'll have ample opportunity in Costa Rica to sort things out.

First, you'll spend several very busy months studying as a trainee. PST will drain and sometimes frustrate you, but you will never be far from helpful Peace Corps staff, a good host family, or your fellow Volunteers. You will start to feel familiar with Costa Rica and begin lasting friendships.

After you swear in, you'll suddenly feel far away from everything. But even in a small town, you'll find no end of people to meet, things to learn, or businesses to chat about. You won't rush to start a killer project to double your town's GDP. Rather, you will take your time to make friends and sound out what projects might be feasible. You will follow your neighbors' cues, whether for teaching children English, advising entrepreneurs, founding a microfinance bank, or teaching a women's group to use Excel. The typical type-A CED volunteer will struggle to adjust to a new pace and style. But you will learn to work independently, set your own goals, design your own projects and—in some ways—be your own boss. And when you've been at your site for a year, it may feel more like home than where you came from.

Life as a PCV will be what you make it. You could manage grants for thousands of dollars or chair a committee on gender and development. You could become a soccer star or organic farmer in your free time. But no matter how you spend your service, you'll leave Costa Rica with marketable skills, personal growth, and experiences you can't find anywhere else.

Sincerely,

Alexander Douglas
Tico 20
Community Economic Development

***

Dear Future Friend,

It's amazing how quickly time has flown. After nearly 18 months of being the lone, spoiled pioneers, Tico 21 TEFL is getting company. I'm sure you've been welcomed and congratulated by several Peace Corps/Costa Rica staff members and Volunteers by this point, but I want to extend a very warm welcome of my own, along with a few words of encouragement and some highly profound Peace Corps wisdom.

Being part of TEFL definitely has its perks. Let me start by saying that. You'll be able to create a schedule with your schools that works for you, affording your life a level of structure that many Volunteers struggle to find. Also, I doubt you'll find yourself defending the validity of your work very often. Inviting native English speakers to help improve a nation's English education program makes sense to people here, and many Costa Ricans are eager to reap the benefits of bilingualism in a country where tourism is a top industry.

I'll be honest though: Being a *TEFLero* has been frustrating for me at times. To practice Spanish I have to be more proactive than I expected, and I've fought the "teacher" label when trying to pursue secondary activities. That being said, my Spanish is just fine, and I've been able to work on all sorts of projects, both TEFL-related and otherwise.

By definition TEFL Volunteers are teachers, but I can assure you that you'll do a great deal of learning while here in Costa Rica. During my time with the Peace Corps I've gained a clearer understanding of my strengths (and fortunately my weaknesses, too), discovered that I can get by without much of what I thought I needed, and grown familiar with a foreign country and culture to a point I never could have imagined. There's one important lesson I still learn daily: As Volunteers, we're equal parts student and teacher, and sometimes the best teachers are really just great guides. A Volunteer's effectiveness isn't measured by the scale of his projects or how swiftly he starts rolling them out. The most fulfilling projects for all involved are those that respond to goals established by the communities we serve, with community members at the helm and Volunteers by their sides. Allow yourself to listen for a while and let your expectations be challenged. Before you can hit your stride you have to understand what a healthy stride looks like.

Serving in the Peace Corps isn't easy, but I imagine you signed up for this expecting it wouldn't be. For me, it's been an incredible journey, and I have a feeling it will be for you, too. Once again, welcome to Peace Corps/Costa Rica! On behalf of the entire TEFL family, we look forward to bringing you into the fold and sharing this experience with you.

Pura Vida,

Bryson Childress, Tico 21
Teaching English as a Foreign Language (TEFL) Volunteer

**

Dear Future Youth in Development Volunteer,

Congratulations on being invited to join us as a Peace Corps Volunteer here in Costa Rica. I know how long and grueling the journey can be to get to this point, and want to commend you for sticking with it. Way to go! As you begin this new chapter in of your life, don't forget to allow yourself to bask in the excitement of this moment and be proud that you have been chosen to serve as a Peace Corps Volunteer.

Costa Rica is an awesome placement! Not because it is "posh corps" (because it isn't) nor because of its beautiful beaches and breathtaking views (definitely perks though). Costa Rica is full of kind-hearted people and a "laid back" way of life. You will find strangers who quickly become family, youth eager to get to know you, communities ready to utilize your skills and expertise, and quite possibly cows blocking your daily route. As a Youth in Development Volunteer you will be working alongside youth leaders, community agencies and local schools. This differs for every volunteer and community, however it could be facilitating art, music or sports activities, co-facilitating sex-education courses, supporting social initiatives (such as drug prevention), or equipping teachers to provide dynamic activities within classroom. Youth in Development Volunteers also support/develop initiatives within the community such as sports teams, art clubs, recreation groups, recycling clubs, etc. The great thing about our job is that the sky is the limit with how we carry out youth development.

Living in a new culture can be challenging, especially thousands of miles away from your friends and family. At times, daily tasks will seem daunting due to possible language barriers, lack of modern conveniences or cultural differences. These moments are real, but with resiliency and perseverance, they will pass quickly; often with a stronger sense of oneself. At times, the realities of working and living in a developing country differ from our expectations. Practicing flexibility and the ability to celebrate small success will be key in helping you overcome these differences.

Being a Peace Corps Volunteer can truly be an incredible adventure. You'll have experiences that you've never even thought of. You will develop deep friendships with both community members and fellow volunteers, and create life-long memories. You will often be the student more than the teacher. Who knows, you may become a master of using a machete, a soccer champion, a "gallo pinto" connoisseur, a coffee bean harvester, or even a recycled materials artist. In all honesty, your experience will be what you make of it. If you come with a willingness to learn and adapt, an open mind, and a spirit of service, you'll do great!

Allow me to offer you a warm welcome from all of us at the PC/CR Youth in Development family!

Pura Vida,
Amanda Bryson
Tico 24

**

Future CED Amigo,

Congratulations! This is very exciting time as you make your first steps into becoming part of the Peace Corps/Costa Rica Volunteer family! It is a very long journey through the application process, so you are to be commended for your dedication. Taking one giant leap out of your comfort zone and into an environment that is not your own, speaking a language that is not your own, and submerged into a culture that is not your own is exhilarating and quite frankly terrifying.

Three months of intensive training is not easy, but it does a great job of preparing you culturally for the road ahead. The Peace Corps staff here in Costa Rica is outstanding and will support you through every step of the way. Try not to be too anxious about site assignment or future projects and just enjoy the *fresquito* air in San Jose and the company of your fellow trainees! They will become your support network over the coming 27 months.

Arriving in site is simultaneously incredibly exciting and entirely overwhelming. Managing your expectations with the unknown is a challenge, but it is a wonderful time to truly invest in your community members. You will learn to be your own boss and to make a schedule that is entirely your own. This responsibility requires the self-motivation to stay active and become engaged. Get out there ever single day. Even if you are just going to the *soda*, or walking door-to-door, attending community *futbol* games, or hanging around the *pulperia*, your first three months in site (when you are completing your community diagnostic) are an excellent time to really build relationships with your neighbors. Hold yourself accountable to having at least one meaningful personal interaction each day and it will benefit you enormously during the stresses and successes of future projects. Having someone to help you one when you can't seem to rally any volunteers or someone to talk to about ideas is a valuable resource. Don't be afraid to put yourself out there. It's not a day in the Peace Corps if you're not looking silly. This experience (like anything) is what you make it, so don't be afraid to push yourself to uncomfortable limits. Learn to laugh at yourself and the comedy and calamity in situations. If you're not having fun, then it's not worth it!

Sustainable development. I thought I knew what that meant before I arrived here in Costa Rica, but the truth is I did not. Sustainability is so much more than reduce, reuse, and recycle. Taking a sustainable approach to grassroots development means not only ensure that initiated projects will continue after you are gone, but it also means investing in individuals. It means investing in the lives of community members so they can work for and amongst themselves in coming decades.

My views of development revolved around infrastructure creation and access to public services. As a CED volunteer, I was sent here to enhance the economy of my site, to help local entrepreneurs, to augment job opportunities to strengthen networks among business owners. Right? Yet one of the most valuable lessons I have learned during my time as a volunteer is that community libraries and computer labs and recycling centers are ineffectual if the community is not invested in their purpose or continued success. If the community does not value reading, they will not value the library. If the community does not connect their current waste behavior with being harmful for the environment, they will not support a recycling center. Grassroots development is not just small-scale development; it is identifying the root of issues and making small changes that enable individuals to create their own success. You must be flexible enough to go where the need is and to build upon what you have.

I have come to truly embrace the old Jerry McGuire "help me help you" approach to my work. Helping your neighbors to help themselves is a wonderful feeling. Being hands on and highly involved at first, and then slowing taking steps back to transition from participant to spectator is a powerful experience. In your two years, you will see changes and see a more independent and self-sustaining community. You will support community members as they develop an idea and turn it into a reality. And of course, inevitably, they will teach you more about life than you teach them about technical skills or project management.

You will be humbled by the realization that you are just one piece to a giant evolving puzzle. Two years seems like a long time now, but the time moves fast and development moves slow. One day you will wake up and know that if you can positively influence the life of just one individual that you will have done your part to better Costa Rica.

Learning yourself (and perhaps relearning yourself) within the parameters of an entirely new experience is certainly a challenge. You will learn how to balance successes and failures, heat and rain, and see beyond your fears and anxieties. This experience will reward you in ways that you could have never expected. You will feel very lonely at times, especially in your community. However, the volunteer network here in Costa Rica is strong and supportive, and you will make friends and build bonds with your fellow volunteers. Together, you will weather the ups and downs of volunteer life. You will celebrate your successes and bounce back from perceived failures. Each volunteer experience is unique in its own right, but if you have been brave enough to make it this far, I know that you will be an excellent Volunteer.

Congratulations on accepting this challenge. I wish you the best of luck during your staging and training, and cannot wait to laugh and share experiences with you.

Sincerely,
Leigh Smith
Tico 24
Community Economic Development

PACKING LIST

This list has been compiled by Volunteers serving in Costa Rica and is based on their experience. Use it as an informal guide in making your own list, bearing in mind that each experience is individual. There is no perfect list! You obviously cannot bring everything on the list, so consider those items that make the most sense to you personally and professionally. You can always have things sent to you later, depending on the climate where you are ultimately placed. As you decide what to bring, keep in mind that you have an 100-pound weight limit on baggage. And remember, you can get almost everything you need in Costa Rica (though it may be somewhat more expensive).

General Clothing

Clothes should be conservative, sturdy, easily washable, and free of the need for ironing, if possible. While it's important to bring practical clothing and special clothing/gear for personal trips and treks (such as quick dry, moisture wick, zip-off pants, etc.), do keep in mind you will be international development professionals, *not* long-term backpackers, hikers, or campers during your two years of service: Your overall attire should reflect this for both professional and security reasons. Volunteers should pack enough for one to two weeks without having to wash clothing. Buying new clothing in Costa Rica is generally cost prohibitive to Volunteers; however, many Volunteers shop at any number of used clothing venues ("Ropa Americana") as an affordable alternative. Women should know that although many Costa Rican women wear short skirts, doing so is likely to attract unwanted attention from men. Most families have washing machines (but not like in the U.S.), clotheslines, and in select few cases spin dryers (no heat), meaning that one's clothing will be stretched or hung out in the sun, causing fading as well. These factors are important when deciding what to bring.

- <u>At least</u> two casual tops (e.g., T-shirts or polo shirts)
- One fleece vest/jacket and one sweater or sweatshirt
- One or two swimsuits
- One lightweight rain jacket or poncho good for going over backpack, bags
- Quality umbrella (it rains almost every day in many parts of Costa Rica during the rainy season)
- Cap or hat for sun protection
- Running gear (if you run)
- Socks (primarily black or white)
- Belts
- Pajamas
- One or two dressy outfits for your swearing-in ceremony or nightlife (on breaks or for workshops)

For Men

- Plenty of pants for work (denim are most common, even in many "professional" settings, but also cotton, khaki, and/or wrinkle-free where possible)
- A variety of shirts, some button-down, some collared (polo and button-down shirts are popular). Most common in rural Costa Rica are short-sleeved button-down shirts, however, long-sleeved is also recommended (If you have tattoos on your forearms, bring a week's worth of long-sleeved shirts because those with tattoos are often mistaken for gang members.)
- Several T-shirts (some Volunteers recommend "easy dry" shirts, finding them to be cooler, easier to dry, and more durable than standard cotton T-shirts in standing up to the weekly washing process)
- One pair of dress pants
- One pair of casual pants (for hiking, painting, etc.)

- Shorts (khaki and athletic) can be used during leisure time in your community, but not in training or professional work environments (schools, offices, etc.)
- Boxers or briefs (at least a week's worth)
- One tie (sport coat optional) for formal occasions/swearing-in

For Women
- Pants for work (denim, cotton, khaki, wrinkle-free)
- Tops for work (T-shirts, blouses, polo shirts, cotton shirts, etc.)
- One pair of dress pants
- Shorts
- Casual skirts or dresses and one or two dressy outfits
- Bras and/or sports tops
- Underwear

Shoes
With the exception of flip-flops, the selection of affordable shoes available in Costa Rica is more limited than in the United States, particularly in larger sizes (over size 9 for women or over size 10-1/2 for men). You may want to bring a two-year supply of shoes. Give preference to shoes that are waterproof and/or can be washed.

- One pair of sturdy walking or tennis shoes
- One pair of running shoes, if you run (It may be challenging to find affordable, quality replacements for running shoes; if you run/exercise a lot consider bringing a second pair or having them sent later.)
- One pair of waterproof hiking boots or Vibram-soled boots (All parts of the country are wet and muddy during the rainy season; note that inexpensive rubber boots that serve the same function can be purchased locally.)
- Two or three pairs of comfortable but nicer/dressier shoes for work and more formal/professional events (can include open-toe shoes/dressy sandals for women)
- Flip-flops or sturdy sandals can be used during leisure time in your community, but not in training or professional work environments (schools, offices, etc.)

Personal Hygiene and Toiletry Items
- Consider regular toiletries (soap, shampoo, shaving cream, body lotion, toothpaste, special floss, etc.). Everything can be found here in-country (prices are slightly higher). If you prefer certain brands, bring them with you, understanding that at some point you'll have to either settle on a locally available brand or pay to have them shipped from the States.
- Any particular brands of over-the-counter medicine you need (the Peace Corps provides some over-the-counter medicine, but usually has only one brand for each type and sometimes they are generic)
- Any homeopathic, macrobiotic treatments or multivitamins you use (the Peace Corps does not provide anything of this nature)
- Fast-drying towels—two bath, one beach, and one hand
- Sunscreen and mosquito repellent, if you have a very strong particular preference for a certain type (the Peace Corps provides one kind of each; mosquito nets are provided)
- Refillable razors (very expensive in Costa Rica)

- Tampons can be found in/around San Jose and major city centers, but they are very expensive. Some female Volunteers recommend bringing a year's supply.
- Hair dryer/straightener (if you use either in the States on a daily basis, you'll probably appreciate having it in Costa Rica)

Miscellaneous
- Two flat sheets or a set for a twin bed (available in-country if you choose not to pack them)
- A favorite pillow and pillowcase(s) (available in-country if you choose not to pack them)
- Flashlight
- Sturdy (larger) backpack or duffel bag for three- to four-day trips (Many Volunteers say this is essential)
- Day pack or small backpack
- Inexpensive water-resistant or waterproof watch
- Small travel alarm clock
- Money belt (optional)
- Leak-proof water bottle/Nalgene
- Pocket knife
- Radio, MP3 player (with electrical cord); favorite DVDs and CDs
- Lint roller
- Scissors
- Start-up supply of stationery, pens, etc. (all such items are available in-country)
- Light sleeping bag (preferably waterproof)
- Camera and film if not digital (camera film is very hard to find/expensive locally)
- A few dollars to use during pre-departure orientation (or staging)
- Photos of family and friends
- Inexpensive jewelry
- Travel games
- A deck or two of playing cards
- Journal
- A pair or two of cheap but strong sunglasses
- Favorite resources for working with children and youth (games, art supplies, icebreakers, etc.)
- Cheap items to use as rewards (e.g., stickers, decorative pencils, or erasers)
- A book or two in English (to read and exchange; Peace Corps/Costa Rica has a library of novels and resource materials) to hold you over until you get into the Peace Corps office
- Rechargeable batteries (regular batteries are available locally, but they are expensive and/or of lower quality)
- Laptop computer (almost all Volunteers find access to a laptop/netbook essential for work and entertainment)
- Locks for luggage
- * Please be advised that the Peace Corps is not responsible for loss or damage to your laptop computer or any other personal articles. Consider taking out personal articles insurance to safeguard against loss or damage.

Items You Do Not Need to Bring

The following items are either available in Costa Rica or provided by the Peace Corps:

- Mosquito net
- Spanish-English dictionary
- Travel books about Costa Rica or Central America (there are plenty in the Peace Corps library)
- Graduate school exam prep books (there are plenty in the Peace Corps library)

PRE-DEPARTURE CHECKLIST

The following list consists of suggestions for you to consider as you prepare to live outside the United States for two years. Not all items will be relevant to everyone, and the list does not include everything you should make arrangements for.

Family

- Notify family that they can call the Peace Corps Counseling and Outreach Unit (COU) at any time if there is a critical illness or death of a family member (24-hour telephone number: 855.855.1961 ext. 1470).

- Give the Peace Corps On the Home Front handbook to family and friends.

Passport/Travel

- Forward to the Peace Corps travel office all paperwork for the Peace Corps passport and visas.

- Verify that your luggage meets the size and weight limits for international travel.

- Obtain a personal passport if you plan to travel after your service ends. (Your Peace Corps passport will expire three months after you finish your service, so if you plan to travel longer, you will need a regular passport.)

Medical/Health

- Complete any needed dental and medical work.

- If you wear glasses, bring two pairs.

- Arrange to bring a three-month supply of all medications (including birth control pills) you are currently taking.

Insurance

- Make arrangements to maintain life insurance coverage.

- Arrange to maintain supplemental health coverage while you are away. (Even though the Peace Corps is responsible for your health care during Peace Corps service overseas, it is advisable for people who have pre-existing conditions to arrange for the continuation of their supplemental health coverage. If there is a lapse in coverage, it is often difficult and expensive to be reinstated.)

- Arrange to continue Medicare coverage if applicable.

Personal Papers

- Bring a copy of your certificate of marriage or divorce.

Voting

- Register to vote in the state of your home of record. (Many state universities consider voting and payment of state taxes as evidence of residence in that state.)

- Obtain a voter registration card and take it with you overseas.

- Arrange to have an absentee ballot forwarded to you overseas.

Personal Effects

- Purchase personal property insurance to extend from the time you leave your home for service overseas until the time you complete your service and return to the United States.

Financial Management

- Keep a bank account in your name in the U.S.

- Obtain student loan deferment forms from the lender or loan service.

- Execute a power of attorney for the management of your property and business.

- Arrange for deductions from your readjustment allowance to pay alimony, child support, and other debts through the Office of Volunteer Financial Operations at 855.855.1961 ext. 1770.

- Place all important papers—mortgages, deeds, stocks, and bonds—in a safe deposit box or with an attorney or other caretaker.

CONTACTING PEACE CORPS HEADQUARTERS

This list of numbers will help connect you with the appropriate office at Peace Corps headquarters to answer various questions. You can use the toll-free number and extension or dial directly using the local numbers provided. Be sure to leave the toll-free number and extensions with your family so they can contact you in the event of an emergency.

Peace Corps Headquarters Toll-free Number: 855.855.1961, press 1, then extension number (see below)

Peace Corps mailing address: Peace Corps
Paul D. Coverdell Peace Corps Headquarters
1111 20th Street, NW
Washington, DC 20526

For Questions About:	Staff:	Toll-Free Extension:	Direct/Local Number:
Responding to an Invitation:	Office of Placement	ext. 1840	202.692.1840
Country Information:	Monica Suber	ext. 2522	202.692.2522
	Desk Officer	msuber@peacecorps.gov	
Plane Tickets, Passports, Visas, or other travel matters:			
	CWT SATO Travel	ext.1170	202.692.1170
Legal Clearance:	Office of Placement	ext. 1840	202.692.1840
Medical Clearance and Forms Processing (includes dental):			
	Screening Nurse	ext. 1500	202.692.1500
Medical Reimbursements (handled by a subcontractor):			800.818.8772
Loan Deferments, Taxes, Financial Operations:		ext. 1770	202.692.1770

Readjustment Allowance Withdrawals, Power of Attorney, Staging (Pre-Departure Orientation), and Reporting Instructions:

	Office of Staging	ext. 1865	202.692.1865

Note: You will receive comprehensive information (hotel and flight arrangements three to five weeks prior to departure. This information is not available sooner).

Family Emergencies (to get information to a Volunteer overseas) *24 hours:*

	Counseling and Outreach Unit	ext. 1470	202.692.1470

www.ingramcontent.com/pod-product-compliance
Lightning Source LLC
Chambersburg PA
CBHW080343290526
45791CB00009BA/2721